# Cash and Working Capital Management

By James O. Onyango

**Thanks a Million!**

Many thanks for purchasing the third of the many eBooks I hope to publish.

The first two are respectively Understanding financial ratios and Understanding Bond markets

I feel honored by your trust and confidence in downloading this eBook!

I hope that you will find it an interesting and useful reading on the management of working capital in the context of short-term financial planning.

Like my first two, this eBook is aimed at those who want a quick read on working capital management but which is discussed in a simple, albeit non-simplistic way, without delving into all the detailed calculations, long formulas and all the technicalities of this important subject.

If you like this eBook please spread the word far and wide.

And, please look out for my next eBook on Understanding Budgetary Control, also coming soon on Kindle Books!

# DEDICATION

To all those accomplished financial experts who have dedicated their careers to making contributions to their companies' strategic decisions in managing working capital, to budding experts and professionals who do not yet realize that their contribution to their company's management of working capital matters and could make a big difference to their company's bottom-line and, to readers everywhere, who, although not necessarily experts in working capital management, at least not yet, are nonetheless, committed to continuous learning as a way of making the world a better place, not just for their companies, experts and themselves, but for the rest of us as well, this eBook is dedicated.

# PREFACE

Working capital management is a critical short–term financial planning issue for all companies. Treasurers and finance directors, must delicately balance the funding of working capital within the business in the long term interest of their shareholders and stakeholders. In **Understanding Working Capital Management,** the author aims to provide a comprehensive introduction to the subject of working capital management from a practitioner point of view with the no, or if at all, minimum quantitative calculations.

It might be argued that much has already been written on the subject of working capital in most financial management text-books. What differentiates **Understanding Working Capital Management** from other books is that it discusses the subject of working capital in a simple and accessible language not normally found in academic textbooks, which tend to be too technical. Like all the other previous publications by this author, this e-book makes the subject of working capital management simple without being simplistic.

In Chapter 1 an introduction to the important subject of financial management and corporate decision-making is discussed in order to provide context for the management of a company's working capital. Also described is the role of finance professionals and the business decisions that these professionals have to make in practice on a day to day basis, including sources of funding. The chapter concludes with a brief overview of the all-important issue critical to shareholders, namely, the dividend policy and what the key drivers of its formulation.

No company can operate successfully without being able to meet its day to day funds requirements and by extension its working capital needs. Short–term financial planning has an important role in this respect. Thus its role in working capital management is discussed in chapter 2. The issues that short – term financial planning seeks to resolve and address together with the challenges to be grappled with in this regard are also discussed in this chapter.

The purpose of Chapter 3 is to describe the key working capital requirements facing any company that wishes to remain competitive and viable in the long-run. In this regard the chapter discusses the key determinants of a company's working capital level. Those responsible for ensuring that funding is available for the company's day to day operations in a cost effective manner need to understand the factors that influence working capital and its importance as the lifeblood of today's organisations and especially its role in the attainment of the organisations long-term financial goals. A discussion of these factors and issues concludes this information loaded Chapter 3.

Chapter 4 presents a detailed discussion of the key financial planning and control issues facing companies in the working capital management space. It synthesizes some of the key working capital issues already discussed in the previous chapter without necessarily being repetitive.

It is important that all the key components of working capital - inventory, accounts receivable and accounts payable are managed by the company in a strategic manner. Accordingly, Chapter 5, 6 and 7 respectively, discusses how each of these components of working capital are strategically managed by company executives, in practice. In these Chapters ways of managing working capital at an optimum level, using various techniques for reducing the amount of inventory that is held, speeding up the collection of receivables and deferring the settlement of payables, are reviewed and discussed.

# ABOUT THE AUTHOR

James Onyango is the Chief Accounting Policy and Research Officer at the African Development Bank, the premier financial institution in Africa, where he is responsible for managing the implementation and application of international financial reporting standards and provision of technical accounting guidance on the financial reporting implications of new and complex treasury products and lending transactions and operations within the Bank. In this role he led the design and assignment of XUA, as the international currency code for the Unit of Account, the reporting currency for the African Development Bank Group, in addition to designing the accounting and reporting framework of the vastly innovative sovereign exposure exchange mechanism among multinational development banks, of which the Bank was part, implemented in 2015.

Previously he worked in the loans accounting and administration division of the Financial Control Department where he not only managed the administration of loans and debt related financial products, but also contributed to the structuring of new and innovative risk-sharing debt products, financial guarantees and loan syndications in a manner which ensures more favourable financial statement reporting effects for the Bank Group.

Before joining the Bank, Mr Onyango worked for several years with the Institute of CPA's of Kenya as the Technical Manager charged with accounting standards setting and continuing professional education. In this role he pioneered the Executive Retreat, the highly popular and cutting-edge seminar for chief executives in addition to developing the first ever accounting practice note offering technical guidance on Auditor's responsibility for financial reports translated from English into Swahili.

Mr Onyango is a Certified Public Accountant and holds a Masters in Accounting and Finance degree from the University of Stirling, United Kingdom. He also holds a Batchelor of Commerce degree majoring in Accounting from the University of Nairobi, Kenya. In addition, Mr Onyango is an Alumnus of the Programme on Investment Appraisal and Management of Harvard University, Cambridge, USA, which he attended in 1994 and an Associate Member of the Association for Certified Fraud Examiners.

## TABLE OF CONTENTS

CHAPTER ONE

FINANCIAL MANAGEMENT AND BUSINESS
DECISONS

**The Financial Decision**

A critical function of financial management in todays' increasingly
competitive and changing business environment is to ensure that there are
adequate funds available for investment in the company's long-term
operational purposes, i.e. for acquiring fixed assets and for short-term
purposes, i.e. as working capital, at all times. As a consequence the
company's financing decision revolves around two main issues, namely,
the amount of funds that is required for investment in the various
operational purposes and the composition of the funds or the sources from
which the requisite funds themselves are to be raised by the company, in a
cost effective manner which assures the long-term business viability of its
operations.

**Capitalisation**

The issue of capitalization has to do with the need to ensure that there is a
balance in the funding of the company. The total amount of funds
available to the company should neither be too much nor too little. An
important question that the company management has to answer is the
question of the capitalization of the company, i.e. the determination of the
amount of funds which the company should have at its disposal - which
will, as noted above, consist of the amount required for investment in

fixed assets and, that portion of working capital which the company must find or raise from its own sources, which will also be out of long-term funds. The total amount of long-term funds available to the company therefore constitutes the capitalization of the company. Let us suppose that a company, Alpha Limited International, has the following balance sheet structure in terms of its financing:

Preference share capital USD 10 million

Equity share capital USD 20 million

Debentures USD 5 million

Loan from African Development Bank USD 5 million

Amount owing to suppliers of goods and services USD 6 million

Based on the above balance sheet Alpha Limited can be said to have long-term funds at its disposal of some USD 40 million. Thus, the amount at which the company can be said to be capitalized is USD 40 million. The capitalisation therefore means the amount of all long-term securities issued by the company including shares and debentures and loans taken from long-term financial institutions, like the African Development Bank, the premier development finance institution in Africa.

Proper capitalization of a company, in the ultimate analysis, will be dependent on the profitability of the company. If the company earns less than what other similar companies earn within the industry, the value of the shares of the company would tend to be rather low and, to that extent the company will likely suffer as its capitalization will be low as well. Let us, suppose, for the sake of argument that a company earns USD 20 million per annum after tax, and investors consider 10% to be the proper after-tax rate of return for similar companies; the capitalisation of the company should then be USD 2 million dollars and not more. Suppose the actual amount of capitalization is USD 2.5 million and the company still earns USD 20 million; its rate of return will be 8% and the investors will not like that. As a result, the shares of the company will then begin to sell at a price lower than other similar companies, for example. In fact, the price will most likely be below par. It may be noted that even if the cost of the fixed assets of a company is more than the proper amount of capitalisation, leading to a lower rate of return, it is still possible for the shares not to fetch a price equal to the par value. This is because for the investor, the cost of the fixed assets is immaterial, for the investor what matters is the yield from the investment. It is therefore important to emphasize, that the amount of proper capitalisation of a company should only be set at a level that is warranted by its level of profits and by the normal rate of return for the industry in which it is operating.

**Over-Capitalisation of the Company**

A company whose total capital, including loans and debentures, exceeds the amount of proper capitalisation as indicated above will be said to be over-capitalised. The one outstanding feature of an over-capitalised company is that its rate of return tends to be lower than that of other similar companies. For listed companies, whenever one finds that the shares of a company are selling at below par, it may be taken to be indicative of a case of an over-capitalised company.

A company should be warry of over - capitalization. There are a number of harmful effects of over-capitalisation, of which the chief ones are the following:

1. The price of the share of the company will be lower than its par value; this means that the shareholders will lose part of their holdings.

2. As a result of the shares selling at below par as indicated above, the investors will not have a good opinion about the company and, should the company require fresh funds, it will find it very difficult to raise these additional funds as no rational investor wishes to invest at a loss.

3. Very often companies resort to questionable practices to artificially inflate their profit, in the short –term, e.g., by not incurring the required advertising expenditure or not carrying out adequate repairs and maintenance of their machinery and or equipment, etc. in order to reduce expenses. This may show the company in good light in the short run but only means that the company's profit - earning capacity in the future will be further damaged leading to even lower profits.

4. Management of over-capitalised companies may adopt many other questionable means of window-dressing their accounts and financial reports so that they may be able to attract investors. This, of course,

borders on fraud and the company may well find itself liable to charges of fraud and mis-representation of fact leading to hefty penalties and fines.

If you would excuse the language, an over-capitalised company can be likened to a very fat person who cannot carry his weight properly. Such a person, as is well known, is likely to be prone to many diseases and certainly not likely to be sufficiently active. An over-capitalised company is in a similar position; unless the condition of over-capitalisation is corrected, the company may find itself in very great difficulties, even in the worst case scenario ending up in bankruptcy.

**Factors Leading to Over-Capitalisation**

What is it that leads a company to end up over-capitalized? There are many contributory factors. The primary factors that contribute to over-capitalisation of a company are highlighted below:

**1. Idle funds**. The company may have some amount of funds that it is not able to use or invest properly. Money may be lying idle in the company's bank accounts or in the form of low yield investments; there may be large inventories or large amounts of debts which the company is not anxious to convert into cash, simply because it has otherwise idle funds lying around. The result of this would be low yield on the capital employed as a whole. Such a company can easily correct its condition of over-capitalisation by either paying off all the loans or even by paying off part of the capital. But the better course would certainly be to try to utilize the funds in some profitable manner. However, this is the only form of over-capitalisation which can be easily corrected.

**2. Overpriced fixed assets.** The fixed assets, especially goodwill, may have been acquired at a cost much higher than that warranted by the service which that asset could render. This may be the result of carelessness or even mischief.

**3. Book value vis-a-vis economic value of fixed assets.** Fixed assets may have been acquired at a time when prices were high. However; with the passage of time prices may have fallen drastically so that the real value of the assets may also have come down substantially, even though in the balance sheet those assets are being shown at their original cost less the depreciation written off. The book value of the fixed assets on the balance sheet may be much more than the economic value.

**4. Inadequate provision of depreciation.** Adequate depreciation may not have been provided for by the company on the fixed assets with the result that the profits shown by its books may have been distributed as dividends, leaving no reserve funds with which to replace the assets at the proper time. Here again the book value of the assets would be much higher than their real economic value.

In short, over-capitalisation in a company results when, either, there is idleness of funds or funds have been lost but their effect has not been recorded or reflected in the books, resulting in a balance sheet which is entirely artificial. The remedy for the latter type of over-capitalisation is to write off the artificial values but also at the same time to pump in more money into the company to make the assets efficient and put them in good working order.

## Under-Capitalisation of the Company

Under-capitalisation is the state of affairs when a company does not have sufficient amount of money at its disposal to carry on its day to day activities. Normally, a forward looking company makes proper arrangements for acquiring fixed assets, through for example, putting aside funds in reserves through depreciation. But the company may not have made adequate arrangements for the working capital either because its estimates were faulty or because the company did not take sufficient care to provide part of the working capital itself through long-term funds. It may also happen that some fixed assets are acquired on hire purchase basis and that, later, instalments are paid out of working capital, depleting the working capital required to run day to day operations in the process. Lack of working capital will create serious consequences for the company. Some of these include:

1. The company will not be able to make purchases on a proper scale causing the company to lose transport economies, trade discounts, etc., leading to higher operating costs and lower profits.

2. The company may not be able to build up proper inventories of finished goods (which may mean lost sales through stock-outs), to extend proper credit to its customers (which may again mean loss of sales) or to have proper cash balances to be able to exploit profitable opportunities that may come up.

3. The company may be forced to forego certain essential expenditures like repairs and maintenance, advertising, etc which will negatively affect its long - term profitability.

4. The company may not be in a position to undertake some activities which are vital for its long-term growth, for example, research and development.

The net effect of all the factors mentioned above will be that the profits of the company will be very low compared to its competitors. Its critical financial ratios, like the turnover ratios, such as sales/inventory, will be very high in the case of under-capitalised companies. If any of these symptoms become evident in the company, the company's management should try to promptly take corrective action by putting in more resources into the company, for it to survive.

**Apparent Under-Capitalisation**
Based on the foregoing discussion of capitalization, it is easy sometimes for it to be argued that since the symptom of an over-capitalised company

is that its shares will sell at below par, a company whose shares sell at a price above par will be under-capitalised. In practice, this is not necessarily true. Both over- and under-capitalized types of companies tend to suffer from low profits and the result would be that the share price would be low. Those companies whose shares sell much above par have hidden strengths or hidden reserves which are not being shown on the balance sheet. For instance, it may be that the company acquired some fixed assets many years ago when prices were low. Today the value of those assets may be very high and the current sales naturally would be made on the basis of current prices leading to very high profits. In the case of such companies the prices of shares would be high. We may term this state of affairs as apparent under-capitalisation since it means that the company is effectively using much more capital than it is showing on the balance sheet.

**Over-Trading and Under-Trading**

Over-trading and under-trading are also facets of under-capitalisation and over-capitalisation. A company which is under-capitalised will try to do too much with the limited amount of capital which it has at its disposal. For example, it may not maintain proper stocks of materials and may depend on regular supplies coming in, say, every week for the production process to go on without negatively affecting the company. Also, it may not extend much credit to customers and may insist only on cash sales. The company may also not pay the creditors on time. One can easily detect cases of overtrading by computing the current ratio and the various turnover ratios of the company. For an overtrading company, the current ratio is likely to be very low but the turnover ratios are likely to be much higher than normally obtains among the companies operating within the industry concerned.

An overtrading company tends to expand too fast. In effect such companies tend to be trade beyond their financial resources. The rapid expansions means that these companies are having to tie up more and more cash in higher and higher levels of stocks and debtors thereby raising their working capital needs rapidly.

Over-trading may also mean entering into too big a commitment for short-selling or buying large stocks in the hope of making a profit when prices move in the right direction. If these operations are not backed by adequate finances, there may be danger since all the company's resources may be wiped off by an adverse movement of prices. An overtrading company can therefore go bust simply because it runs out of cash to pay its day to day bills, even though it may have been operating at a profit.

Over-trading as a whole is dangerous for a company because, once the chain breaks, it may mean the complete collapse for the business. If, for instance, the overtrading company has issued cheques to creditors, hoping that these will be presented to the bank only after a week and in the meantime amounts will be deposited in the bank after collection from debtors that will make it possible for the cheques to be honoured, and if, for any reason, the expected amounts cannot be collected or are not deposited, the cheques to the creditors will be returned dishonoured with all the undesirable consequences.

Due to the concerns about the consequences of overtrading investment analysts therefore always check the company's accounts to see if a company has adequate resources to finance its business and whether it would be able to raise any additional money needed for its operations.

Under-trading is the reverse of over-trading. Under-trading means the company is actually keeping funds idle and not using them properly to build the business. Keeping large inventories, large amounts of book debts, large cash balances, low amounts due to creditors, etc. are all indicative of under-trading.

The symptom to look for in the case of under-trading would be a very high current ratio and very low turn-over ratios. Under-trading is an aspect of over-capitalisation and ultimately leads to low profits. The proper remedy to under-trading is to use the available funds where they can earn reasonable profits for the company, say, by starting another line of production.

**Sources of Company Financing**

The question of sources of funds for a company is one of the most important questions for any treasurer or finance manager of any business enterprise to address and deal with in their financial management role.

Sources of funds for a company has to be, necessarily examined from the undermentioned standpoints:

- **Availability of funds for the proper duration**. Short-term funds like bank credit cannot be used for acquiring fixed assets for which purposes the source should be such that the demand for repayment or return will not be made before the company is able to collect the funds through operations—in case of fixed assets, the process of collection is chiefly the depreciation provision. Short-term funds are usually less costly than long-term funds. Therefore, except to the extent necessary, a company should not use long-term funds for short-term purposes. Management should therefore do whatever is necessary to ensure that it is always only making a proper use of bank credit at its disposal.

- **Effect of the financing source on the cost of capital**. Because of income-tax, the cost of borrowed funds is usually much lower than that of equity funds. Hence too much dependence on equity funds will raise the cost of capital or the cut off rate for investment. Too much dependence on borrowing, will tend to make the lenders charge a higher rate of interest to the company.

- **Debt-Equity ratio**. Investors do not look with favour on companies where the proportion of long-term loans to total capital employed is too high or too low, considering the average in the industry concerned. In such a case, the price of the shares is likely to be lower because of the lower price earnings (PE) ratio or the higher expected rate of return.

- **Flexibility.** A company should be in such a position as to be able to take advantage of all profitable opportunities that may come its way. Sometimes, for want of finances, it may not be able to do so. Suppose a company wants to raise funds for acquiring another business but its debt-equity ratio is already as high as is permissible. In this case, the company may be forced to issue equity shares which it may not like to or which investors may not be willing to subscribe to. The financial structure should be such as to enable the company to raise further funds as necessary, without strain.

- **Interference of providers of financing in the management of the company**. New equity shares may mean new shareholders with full voting rights which, in turn, may mean that the present management team may no longer be able to work without interference. Financing through loans has the advantage that the management team or the Board of Directors is not disturbed in the exercise of their discretion in managing the company. However, too much dependence on loans may also compel the company to accept representatives of the lenders on the Board of Directors. From the point of view of the two points made above, it is desirable that the company should retain for its own use a large part of profits earned. Retained profits are part of the company's equity permitting further borrowing without upsetting the company's debt-equity ratio and without thus forcing outsiders on management.

- **Market sentiment**. The sentiment in the capital market is always changing. Sometimes investors want only equity shares and sometimes they only want debentures. Sometimes the market is so sluggish that securities cannot be issued in a timely manner and funds can be raised only from financial institutions. This factor is of obvious importance in raising the required financing for company operations; the company may not like what the investors want but if it wants funds, the investors' terms must be met.

Other than loans and debentures, preference shares have not been mentioned in the discussions above, as a source of funding for companies. There is a good reason for this. Preference shares are not much in favour with either companies or investors since they are considered, to use an animal kingdom analogy, to be neither fish nor fowl, or for batman fans, as more of a bat who in African folklores is disowned by both the mammals and the birds. For the company, a dividend paid on a preference share is a moral must (though legally a company may refuse to pay the dividend) without the advantage of tax which is available in case of a payment of debenture interest. Preference shareholders may get a dividend slightly higher than the interest obtaining on debentures but their security is much less than that of debenture-holders. Also, there are almost no prospects of capital appreciation in the prices of preference shares.

When push comes to shove, a company will always have another financing source, even if all other sources dry up - the amount representing accumulated depreciation provision. This is like retained profits, even though it will not be counted as part of equity, and can certainly be used for long-term purposes. Companies always take into account the total cash inflow when they plan operations; cash inflow of course means profit after tax plus depreciation.

**The Dividend Decision:**

This another critical financial management decision facing company treasurers. The decision as to how much dividend should be paid out to the company's shareholders has to be made by the management chiefly by reference to two factors, already to yield:

(i) the yield that the company will be able to get, if it uses the funds concerned in making investments; and

(ii) the yield that the shareholders will be able to get, if the profit is distributed to them as dividend and they decided to invest the funds themselves.

As a general rule, the company should retain and invest the funds itself if it can earn more than what the shareholders would be able to earn if the profit was distributed to them as dividend. Because of the income-tax which shareholders have to pay on dividends' and because of the difficulty of ascertaining the marginal rate of income tax for the average shareholder, the company is usually justified in retaining profits for its own use in expanding the business, if a reasonable cash dividend is paid.

**Dividend Policy Choices**

There are a number of policies and practices which the company may adopt in respect of dividends.

These policies include, but are not limited to, the following:

(i)    The company may pay a fixed dividend every year on its shares, irrespective of the amount of the profit earned. If the profits earned are very high and get accumulated, later bonus shares are issued but the rate of dividend per share is maintained. In this case the pay-out ratio, i.e., the ratio of total dividend paid to total profit earned, will change from year to year.

(ii)   The company may pay a fixed proportion of profits earned as dividend. In this case, the rate of dividend per share will fluctuate from year to year.

(iii)  The company may consider the question of how much dividend to pay afresh each year so that the rate of dividend per share and even the pay-out ratio may change from one year to another. If the company's profits rise, the dividend is likely to be increased. But there is no guarantee that there will be dividend at all. If the company makes losses, it may well have to cease paying a dividend.

Of the above three policies, the first practice is usually much more preferred by both companies and investors since investors are certain of the return that they will get from their investment in the company.

**Factors Influencing Dividend Policy**

The factors that a company should consider while formulating and framing its dividend policy are the following:

**The wishes of investors.** Big and rich shareholders do not like cash dividend since in their case the rate of income-tax is very high. Since the rate of tax on capital gains is usually lower than that on income, such shareholders want the value of the shares to appreciate which it will if the company uses the funds profitably. However, there are numerous shareholders, like old and retired people, who depend on dividend income for their day-to-day living expenses. Such shareholders want a cash dividend. Also, institutional investors like a cash dividend since they themselves have to pay dividend or interest to their own investors. Each company must try to ascertain the wishes of its shareholders and act accordingly.

**Effect of dividend on Price Earnings (PE) Ratio.** The PE ratio is likely to be rather low in case of a company which does not pay a reasonable cash dividend (after all unless cash dividend is paid, how can one be sure of the figure of profit disclosed by the financial statements?) and which does not pay dividend regularly. For maintaining share prices and for raising them, the payment of a regular dividend at a certain level is essential.

**Company's own funds requirements.** If the company needs funds itself in order to expand operations, obviously it will try to retain as large a portion of the profit as possible. And conversely, if a company has no investments in which it can profitably use excess funds, it would be better to pay out the profit to shareholders as dividend rather than keep the funds idle.

**Effect of dividend payout on working capital.** Sometimes, payment of dividend may mean depletion of the company's working capital leading to adverse effects on the business operations. If this is the case then, the management should then be bold enough to refuse to pay dividend. However, if the payment of dividend affects working capital to such an extent, the company management need to be aware that the figure of profit itself will be questionable, unless the rationale for the company's decision is well explained and accepted by the investors.

**Contingencies.** A company must maintain reserves, usually referred to as capital reserves, to meet unforeseen contingencies and losses. This is of special importance to newly established concerns since they cannot look to outside help if they find themselves in difficulties. Shareholders of a new company do not normally expect a dividend for the first few years.

The company should take advantage of this grace period, so to speak, and build up large reserves as quickly as possible before the honeymoon, to borrow from a marriage analogy, is over.

It is very important to keep in mind the fact that, really no profit is earned till the pay-back period of the fixed assets is safely over, even though the profit and loss account may reveal a profit. Suppose an asset somehow has to be discarded before the pay-back period, the book value of the asset must be written off and that will convert the so-called profit into a loss. From this point of view also, it would be better not to pay out the profit earned for a few years as dividend in order to build a financial buffer.

**Role, Duties and Responsibilities of Financial Manager/ Treasurer**

Apart from the three broad functions of financial management mentioned above, the financial manager or Treasurer, or however called, has to perform certain routine functions.

The duties and functions include:

(i) Keeping track of actual and projected cash inflows and cash outflows and making adequate provisions in time for any shortfall that may arise.

(ii) Managing of cash resources centrally and ensuring that the financial needs of various divisions and departments of the company are well supplied without keeping idle cash at many points.

(iii) Negotiations and management of banking and business relations with banks and other financial institutions.

(iv) Investment of excess funds available and free for a short period.

(v) For listed companies, keeping track of stock exchange prices in general and prices of the company's shares in particular.

(vi) Maintenance of liaison with production and sales departments for ensuring that working capital position is not upset because of inventories, book debts, etc.

(vii) Keeping management informed of the financial implications of the various developments in and around the company.

# CHAPTER TWO

Short-term financial planning by definition covers a shorter planning time horizon and is aimed at meeting the company's budgetary, financial and investment goals within one fiscal year or a shorter period as compared to long - term plans which cover a planning and operational time horizon of more than one year. Naturally, short - term plans tend to have a higher degree of certainty compared to long-term plans. Since short term financial plans tend to facilitate the management by companies of their short-term cash deficits they are often amended regularly as the strategic, financial and investment goals of the business change.

In the preparation of short term plans there are critical business issues that must be addressed. Accordingly, short-term financial planning involves considering and answering questions which address the following issues:

- The appropriate level of cash that the business needs to keep on call and short notice at various dates during the next planning period
- The optimal level of inventory that the company needs to maintain
- The frequency and timeliness of paying off the bank overdraft

- The period of credit that the company should grant to its customers and or debtors for sales made on credit
- Whether the company's suppliers or creditors in this case, should be paid more quickly than currently in order to take advantage of the cash discount being offered.
- The proportion of the company's current assets which should be financed by short-term funds
- What working capital is and what influences its level.

Short-term financial planning is concerned with what is referred to as working capital. Working capital can be defined as the excess of current assets over current liabilities. It is the same as net current assets. It represents the investment of a company's funds in assets which are expected to be realized within a relatively short period of time. Working capital is not an investment in an asset with a long life but, as the name implies, it represents funds which are continually in use by the company and are turned over many times in a year. It is the capital used to finance production, to support levels of stock and to provide credit for customers. The three main current assets are stock or inventory, debtors (accounts receivables), and cash. These current assets can be funded by short-term finance, i.e. current liabilities, or by medium - and long-term finance.

The working capital is derived by the following formula:

Working capital = cash + debtors + stock - short-term liabilities

Working capital can also simply be defined as Current assets less Current liabilities.

It should be noted that the more of a business's finance is invested in working capital, the less is available for investing in long-term assets such as buildings, plant and machinery. It is generally believed that the profits to be earned from investing **in** long-term assets are greater than the profits to be earned from investing in current assets. As a consequence the company should strive to minimize its own investment in working capital and to concentrate its resources on investments with a longer life than current assets, with as much as is safe of the current assets being financed by current liabilities.

However, in some economic conditions the wisdom of the day may suggest that it is better for a business to keep its resources liquid by investing them in working capital via the current assets, including placing any surplus cash into short-term financial investments. It is argued that at certain times it is possible for the returns from longer-term investments, in plant and machinery say, to be less than those from short-term financial investments. It can be argued that being liquid enables the business to take immediate advantage of any financial opportunity that may arise, e.g. opportunities available in the stock market or money market.

At times, it is certain that the returns from investing in plant and machinery required in the manufacturing industry have appeared unattractive relative to the returns on short-term investments. However, it has to be recognized that, from the point of view of the overall economy, somebody needs to manufacture the goods or products so that others can trade.

The manager's objective in short-term planning is to maintain sufficient cash on hand or on short call to meet any normally predictable expenses without resorting to costly emergency measures. Ideally, the Manager will gauge matters so finely that he never actually has more cash on hand than will be needed, because surplus cash is an idle asset and as such it incurs an opportunity cost – that is, the cost to the company of what it could earn if the same funds were invested elsewhere in securities or long-term deposits.

There is a danger that with inflation, any money invested in monetary assets is losing value. Normally the higher the rate of inflation the lower should be the cash balances maintained at the firm.

The extent to which cash is put to effective use within the business will reflect agreeably on the company's profit levels. However, there are limits. The loss of liquidity due to maintaining very low cash balances and not having overdraft arrangements could lead the company into difficulties. Slowness in paying debts may mean that cash discounts are forfeited or, perhaps more seriously, that suppliers are lost. The key to the management of cash and of all working capital is therefore a matter of striking a delicate balance between risk and profitability.

This can be a complex procedure. For instance, it is possible for a company to become insolvent while it is still recording profits, because profits are calculated on the accrual system of accounting whereas liquidity is a matter of cash flow. Therefore, while a sale may be 'made' and recorded in the year-end accounts, the actual liquidity position of the company is unimproved unless the purchaser has paid by the end of the year.

The traditional accounting statements — the balance sheet and the profit and loss account —are the results of the accrual system of accounting. In an accrual accounting system, expenses are charged to the period in which the goods usage or services are received, which is not necessarily the period in which expenses are paid. For example, wages are normally paid in arrears, and if accounts are to be prepared at a date which is in the middle of a week, the services of the employees will have been received and the expenses will therefore be recognized in the accounts although the wages have not yet been paid.

Similarly, income is recognized with accrual accounting when a sale has been made, or when interests or dividends are due, which is not necessarily when the income is received. It has been said that any fool can sell an item, but the good salesman is identified by the fact that the customers pay up at the right time. A number of companies still operate as part of their performance management system, the bonus system whereby the salesman is rewarded for making the sale. It might be more prudent in some situations to have a performance incentive system where the company distribute the bonuses as and when the cash has been collected. It depends whether responsibility lies as much with the salesman as with the finance department. The accrual system of accounting and the treatment of items such as capital expenditures and long-term contracts can cause a problem in the interpretation of company accounts and in setting up appropriate performance incentives.

However, the fact that there are difficulties in identifying the profit of a company for a period of time, and that this profit figure must depend upon certain assumptions, need not interfere with cash management. When cash comes into a business and when it leaves the business is not a matter of interpretation but a matter of fact. Successful management of working capital or cash depends upon knowledge of the cash flow position of the company.

From the foregoing discussion it is clear that the problems and challenges of short-term financial management are as complex as those which beset long-term financial planning.

# CHAPTER THREE

## UNDERSTANDING WORKING CAPITAL REQUIREMENTS

From the discussion in the previous chapters it is abundantly clear that working capital, and its proper management is very vital for the successful operation of any company. This is because, as already explained, working capital represents the funds and resources that is required for the day to day running and operation of the company. No company can operate successfully without being able to meet its day to day funds requirements and by extension its working capital requirements.

In a company's day to day operations it requires working capital for maintenance of inventories, in the case of a trading company, for extending credit to customers and for maintaining an appropriate cash balance. This means the working capital requirement needs of a company can be met from external and internal sources - partly by the credit that the company is able to negotiate with its suppliers of goods and services with the rest of the working capital needs being met from the internal resources of the company like its cash balance, for example. Since working capital is required for effective day to day operations the company management must pay close attention to the amounts it has invested in various forms of current assets within the business as this is what helps fuel, so to speak the business operations. In fact without working capital the company's fixed assets would be quite useless. Indeed the company must ensure that it maintains an optimal balance in its investments in working capital because holding resources in working capital is not costless.

An excessive investment by a company in working capital, at any point in time, is likely to have a negative impact on the results of its operations. The company could suffer the following losses due to its investment in excess working capital levels:

- Interest that the company has to pay to the Bank
- Interest it loses which it would otherwise have earned by keeping the cash or funds in the Bank
- The opportunity cost represented by profits it would have earned by putting the excess funds invested in working capital into alternative uses or alternative investments.

For the above reasons, it is imperative for management to ensure that the working capital level that it maintains earns it at least as much return as the funds would have earned had they been invested elsewhere. In making this strategic trade-off the company needs to ensure it does not necessarily starve itself of working capital given the importance of working capital in the utilization of the fixed assets at the company's disposal which would otherwise be impossible. Actually it is for this reason that when the company is considering the acquisition of fixed assets, as part of its capital budgeting, it has to look at the total investments it has made, not just in the fixed capital but also the total amount of working capital that will be required to keep the fixed assets in operation

Each of the working capital items or components, and hence the level of working capital are influenced by various factors. When considering the control of receivables (debtors), accounts payable (creditors) and stocks it is possible to calculate ratios which can be used to monitor movements in these items. For example, the average length of credit being allowed on debtors can be determined from calculating the ratio of debtors to sales.

Purchases, and consequently the credit figure, are made up of a mixture of items including; materials for stock; materials for consumption; wages and salaries; payment for services, energy, rent; purchase of capital equipment etc.

It is not possible to find an effective measure of volume for purchases, and so control ratios for payables cannot easily be calculated. However, it is possible to observe the movements in the creditors' figure on a week-by-week basis or a month-by-month basis. Any unusual changes can be examined on an item-by-item basis. Relevant questions can then be asked.

Of course the type of working capital required can vary from one industry to another. These industry differences have to be allowed for in any comparisons being made across companies. What is an acceptable financial position in, say, the retailing industry would not be acceptable in a manufacturing industry.

A retailing company usually has high levels of finished goods stock and very low levels of debtors. Most of the retailer's sales will be for cash, and even sales on credit are usually handled by an independent credit card company or a financial subsidiary of the retail business. The retailing company, however, usually has high levels of creditors. It pays its suppliers after an agreed period of credit. The levels of working capital required are therefore low. In fact, they can be very low, with some retailers having high levels of short-term borrowing.

In contrast, a manufacturing company will require relatively high levels of working capital with investments in raw materials, work in progress and finished goods stocks, and with high levels of debtors or receivables. The credit terms offered on sales and taken on purchases will be influenced by the normal contractual arrangements in the industry.

To determine the level of cash that a company requires it is necessary to prepare a cash budget where the minimum balances needed from month to month will be defined. If expenditures are lumpy or the business is seasonal, cash shortages may arise in certain periods. Generally it is thought better to keep only sufficient cash to satisfy short-term needs, and to borrow if longer- term requirements occur. Maintaining a very large cash balance to meet every eventuality likely to arise throughout the planning period is thus discouraged in favour of *ad hoc* borrowing, based on the company's financial needs. The problem, of course, is to balance the cost of this borrowing against any income that might be obtained from investing the cash balances. Since cash needs can hardly ever be predicted with absolute certainty, some firms will no doubt opt for a safety stock of cash with which to meet the unexpected. Like any other insurance premium this particular brand of peace of mind involves an opportunity cost.

The difficulty of pinpointing the 'right' level for cash is a theme with variations. Many attempts have been made to develop a model for the control of cash. The famous square-root inventory model has been applied in theory to the problem of determining an optimal level of cash. This is, however outside the scope of this discussion.

The size of the cash balance that a company might need depends on the availability of other sources of funds at short notice, the credit standing of the company and the control of debtors and creditors - a crucial factor for short-term financial planning. The flow of cash in and out of the business can, to some extent, be controlled by such tactics as speeding up the collection of debts (perhaps by offering an attractive discount to buyers), factoring debts, or delaying disbursements of cash to creditors.

The debtors or receivables problem that companies face again revolves around the choice between profitability and liquidity. It might, for instance, be possible to increase sales by allowing customers more time to pay, but since this policy would reduce the company's liquid resources it would not necessarily result in higher profits. Often the terms of sale are dictated by common practice within the industry; if not, the company can design its own terms with a view to regulating the level of debtors. As result a company is actually free to exercise some judgement in the matter of its customers and can therefore control the total risks attached to its sales, assuming, of course, that it is possible through historical analysis or the use of established credit ratings for the company to classify groups of customers in terms of credit risk. As the company's sales output changes in relation to capacity the company may choose to change its credit policy to ensure some level of strategic alignment. In some industries certain firms devote generous sums to the machinery of debt collection, sometimes with significant results.

If a company has a short-term liquidity problem it can resort to invoice discounting or factoring. These measures, once regarded so unfavorably by many companies, are now becoming accepted particularly among rapidly expanding small - or medium-sized firms whose growth would normally be hampered if large amounts of capital were tied up in book debts. A proportion of the company's book debts can be converted into cash by discounting through the services of a specialized finance company. Three-quarters of the value of sales invoices can be advanced in return for a bill of exchange for future payment of the advance plus interest. As discussed in a later chapter, factors provide added services in respect of accounts receivables management, such as purchase of all the client's invoiced debts and the arrangement of all debtor control, debt collection and sales ledger accounting. It is even possible to have an undisclosed factor, of whose operations as a third party the buyer is quite unaware since under most of the conventional factoring arrangements he pays his debts to the seller in the conventional manner. In this situation, in fact, the seller actually collects the debts on behalf of the factor. All these services have a cost, but for companies short of working capital the ensuing benefits may well justify the cost.

The management of inventories is as important for the company's short-term financial situation as the management of cash, and again a balance has to be found: this time between tying up money which is not earning anything and losing sales, and profits as result of not being able to meet an order from a customer when it is received. Thus there is always need for adequate inventory or stocks. Clearly, to be quite certain that no customer ever has to wait for any but the shortest time between placing an order and receiving the delivery of the goods and that in the case of manufacturing concerns, that there is no machine that is idle because raw materials are not available, large stocks must be held. Large stocks give security against interruption of the sales or manufacturing process.

Of course, the larger the level of stocks that are held by the company, the less the risk of disappointing customers or of experiencing hold –ups on the production process, but idle stocks cost money. Goods and stocks on the shelves rather than already sold represent working capital tied up and not available for reinvestment by the company in new supplies of raw materials or for other uses. To be sure every USD 1 worth of excess inventory held by the company represents a real cost to the business because of the loss of the earning power of the tied - up capital.

The other side of the working capital problem concerns obtaining short-term funds. Every source of finance, including taking credit from suppliers, has a cost; the point is to keep this cost to the minimum. The cost involved in using trade credit might include forfeiting the discount normally given for prompt payment, or loss of goodwill through relying on this strategy to the point of abuse. Some other sources of short-term funds are bank credit, overdrafts and loans from other institutions. These can be unsecured or secured, with charges made against inventories, specific assets or general assets.

The short-term financial planning problem that companies face is really that of balancing the options. Cash requirements with seasonal patterns involve deciding whether to use short-term funds, take credit, offer varying discounts, employ factors to liquidate the debt or maintain large balances. Given the forecasting requirements and the alternative costs, it is theoretically possible to make an optimal decision.

# CHAPTER FOUR

## WORKING CAPITAL PLANNING AND CONTROL

From the previous chapter we have noted that working capital can be defined as the money or resources tied up in inventory and receivables from debtors less the amounts payable to creditors. For most product-based businesses, the amount of money and resources tied up in working capital can be substantial. For example, a look at the balance sheet of many large multinational companies will show billions of dollars of their resources tied up in inventory, receivables and total debt with millions of dollars being paid out by the companies by way of interest on their debts in any given year. This means that if these companies could reduce the levels of their inventory and receivables, they could substantially eliminate some of their debt and related interest costs.

The management and control of a company's working capital is critical to its long term financial success and business sustainability. The company's Financial Manager or Treasurer can use a wide variety of approaches in undertaking working capital planning and control. These approaches range from the use of simple rule of thumb methods, to more sophisticated mathematical and computer models.

The simple approach relies on keeping working capital levels within certain limits, determined by financial ratio analysis. A number of the commonly used financial ratios can be applied in this regard. The ratio analysis approach is based on the idea that working capital should be funded in one way and long-term assets funded in another way. In general, to fund long-term assets with current liabilities would be seen as dangerous, and to fund non-permanent working capital with long-term funds would be seen as a waste. This financial ratio analysis approach is often found in practice in many companies: the disadvantage is that the financial ratios used as guides controlling working capital are themselves to some extent merely rules of thumb. However, at any point in time there are a set of generally accepted levels for certain financial ratios which can be useful as a guide for planning and control purposes.

The financial manager must always assess the long - and short - term financing and funding problems in terms of the company's capital structure as a whole. This is important as in any case, others will certainly be doing so: the investment analysts who can affect the cost of capital for a company by their interpretation of the company's financial strength and growth possibilities make use of financial ratios, as do other companies, banks and credit agencies who have business dealings with the company, when deciding whether to advance a company some credit and or short-term loans. Due to the perceived usefulness of financial ratios by business decision - makers, the criticisms of theorists who regard financial ratios as arbitrary rules of thumb, have fallen largely on deaf ears among the prac-titioners. It is true that other factors are considered, but the role of financial ratios in the control of working capital cannot be ignored.

One other way to approach the problem of calculating working capital needs, is to ascertain the funds required to support an extra dollar's worth of sales. It is quite possible for a company which is profitable, growing, with no capacity constraint, and with no need for new fixed investment to still have a financing problem.

One fairly accurate way of estimating working capital needs is to first determine the relationship between debtors and sales, creditor and sales and inventory and sales. Starting with the company's budget which shows the expected increase in sales over the next period, for example, it is possible to use the relationship determined between sales and the relevant items of current assets and current liabilities to estimate the level of extra working capital needed to finance the extra expected increase in sales.

The working capital cycle  or turnover measures how effective the company  is in managing the cash tied up in its day to day operations and involves moving for example from cash to supplier to inventory through the customer and then back to cash and to supplier and so on. In other words cash is paid to a supplier who provides inventory. Thus the working capital cycle starts with the purchase of inventory. The inventory is converted to finished goods and held in the warehouse until purchased by a customer. The customer pays for the goods which brings cash back into the business. Both suppliers and customers have credit terms, so the key factor is how long cash stakes to complete the cycle. Money tied up in this cycle has to be funded and can be significantly drain the resources required for investment in assets.

There is often a raging debate about whether cash should be included or excluded as part of working capital. Those who argue for the exclusion of cash often cite the fact that cash is not, strictly speaking, "working" for the business, it is normal to exclude it from the calculation of working capital and limit the definition of working capital to just the three trading items of inventory, receivables and payables.

The common measures used to monitor the levels of these assets and liabilities are basically the day measures: inventory is measured by the number of days it is held for resale; receivables by the number of days it takes to collect cash; and payables by the number of days a business waits before settling its accounts with suppliers. The aim of effective working capital management is to minimise the number of days taken for cash to complete the cycle – that is to move from cash into supplier inventory and then into inventory to the customer and back into cash.

The number of days for cash to complete the cycle is determined by the formula: Inventory days + Receivables days — Payables days.

It is possible to create "negative" working capital where inventory levels are low, sales are all in cash, thereby creating no receivables in the company's balance sheet while taking full advantage of credit from the company's suppliers.

Based on the foregoing working capital can be made negative by receiving money from customers in advance of paying suppliers. Mathematically this means the amount of payables is greater than the amount of inventory and receivables combined This structure is found in airlines, insurance companies, supermarkets and food retailers and generates cash for the business, which can be used to fund property and equipment.

The working capital cycle needs to be optimized based on the specificities of the business and the company's long-term goals.

The optimization of the working capital cycle is measured by the working capital turnover which is computed by dividing revenue by working capital top give a value which is a multiple. This means that as the working capital becomes leaner the multiple will increase thereby increasing the working capital turnover, illustrating the efficiencies that have been gained. If the business manages to reduce working capital still further until it becomes negative, the additional improvements will be delivered by a decrease in the ratio, showing that more cash has been released.

**Factors Determining the Working Capital**

Issues and challenges facing companies with regard to management of working capital differ based on the circumstances of the company. In general the following factors determine the amount and scale of the working capital that is required by a company at any point in time.

- Nature of the industry
- Demand within the industry
- Cash requirements of the company
- Nature of the company's business - whether cyclical or seasonal
- Manufacturing time
- Volume of sales
- Financial terms applicable to the company's purchases and sales
- Inventory turnover
- Business turnover
- Business cycle
- Current assets requirements
- Production cycle
- Credit control  posture of the company as demonstrated by the applicable terms and conditions
- Inflation or price level changes
- Profit planning and control
- Repayment ability of the customer
- Cash reserves held by the company
- Operational efficiency
- Change in technology
- Firm's finance and dividend policy
- Attitude towards risk whether conservative or liberal

**Forecasting and Estimation of Working Capital Requirements**

This is a very important factor in the planning and control of a company's working capital.

Factors to be considered in forecasting working capital requirements include the following:

- **Cost**. Total costs incurred on materials, wages and overheads
- **Time**. The length of time for which raw materials remain in stores before they are issued to production.
- **Production cycle**. The length of the production cycle or work in progress, i.e., the time taken for conversion of raw materials into finished goods.
- **Sales cycle**. The length of the Sales Cycle during which finished goods inventory are to be kept waiting before sales they are sold for cash or on credit.
- **Credit period for customers**. The average period of credit allowed to customers.
- **Expense cash requirements**. The amount of cash required to pay day-to-day expenses of the business.
- **Advance cash requirements**. The amount of cash required for advance payments if any.
- **Credit period by suppliers**. The average period of credit to be allowed by suppliers.
- **Time - lag**. The time - lag in the payment of wages and other overheads.

In the following Chapters ways of managing working capital at an optimum level, using techniques for reducing the amount of inventory that is held, speeding up the collection of receivables and deferring the settlement of payables, is reviewed and discussed.

# CHAPTER FIVE

## STRATEGIC MANAGEMENT OF INVENTORY

**Inventories and Stocks**

Inventories and stocks are vital for a trading company. Of course this is less so for a service company, like a bank, offering financial services. For a trading company inventories consist of raw materials in stock, work in progress and stock of finished goods which are ready for sale. Each of these has a different function to perform in the business and all concerned with their management must keep in view the functions when allocating funds for the purposes of keeping the optimal level of inventory and stock within the company at each point in time. Each of the three components of inventories and stock are discussed below. We begin with raw materials and its function in the business.

**Raw materials**

The key function of raw materials in the business is to enable production to be carried out smoothly and at a sufficient level to be able to service the customers demand. However, in the case of rising prices, as has been the case in many parts of the world in recent years, raw materials stocks have another function to perform, namely, insuring that costs will be kept under control as far as possible.

There are two types of costs which are involved in acquiring materials and stores and in keeping them in stock within the company. The first type of cost is the cost of placing an order and receiving the goods. The larger the number of orders placed the larger the level of the costs involved is expected to be. The second type of cost is the one involved in keeping the item in stock. This cost usually consists of the interest on the capital which is locked up in the stock, the possible deterioration in quality of the stock and the risk of obsolescence, etc. In any effective inventory management system, in normal times, the objective should be to minimize the total of the two types of costs mentioned above.

Companies can deploy various ways of minimizing the two types of inventory costs. One popular approach is normally to manage the stock on the basis of what is called selective inventory control or the ABC system. ABC System involves dividing the items on the inventory in any company into three categories – A, B and C! In every company one is likely to find a small number items but which taken together will usually involve a good deal of investment. Such items may be termed as "A" category. On the other extreme the company may have a large number of items involving rather small investment of funds. These items may be termed category C items. And in between A and C there is another category which may be termed "B"- involving moderate levels of investment. After determining the categories the company has to apply an appropriate stock management strategy with the company's stock management strategy varying depending on the category of the assets involved.

**Strategy for each Category of Inventory**

With respect to 'C" items it is better for the company to place a very big order once since this will mean saving the cost of repeated orders and not incurring much higher costs for storing the goods since the investment is small.

In the case of category B stock items where the investment is not too large as that of category A, orders for replenishment of stocks should be placed on a review basis with the stock records being reviewed thoroughly each month, and if based on the review, the stock seems to be rather low, another order is placed. For items in category A, a more vigorous and close stock or inventory monitoring, management and control regime is necessary.

**Control of Stock Inventory**

Below are the different stock control issues surrounding smaller category of items but which involve a good deal of huge investment:

- Fixing the minimum limit to ensure that supplies will always be available. This is usually done on the basis of the consumption in the lead-time that will elapse between the time of placing the order and the actual receipt of the goods plus margin of safety.
- Fixing the maximum limit above which without prior sanctions the actual stock should not be allowed to rise.
- Determining the economic order quantity that is the optimum quantity that should be ordered at one time.

**Maximum Stock Inventory**

In setting up the maximum stock or inventory limit that should be maintained the company must consider the following factors:

- The amount of funds and storage space available
- Future production plans of the company which will ensure that the quantity which is likely to be in stock will be actually required for production. If the product or the material is to be changed, the stock naturally should be kept at a low level
- The conditions of supply. If it is anticipated that difficulties will develop in the availability of materials, large stocks will generally be maintained.
- Expected rise in the price of materials or in the price of the finished goods. In this case also rather large stock holdings will be maintained since the cost of maintaining large stocks in storage may be less than the rise in prices.

From a strategic standpoint, it is important to note that all limits on stock levels whether maximum or minimum are subject to constant review so that changing conditions are always kept in mind and adjusted for, as necessary. Constant action is also required to see that all slow moving stocks items or all obsolete items are disposed of as quickly as possible. There is often much inertia in this respect and one can often see large numbers of items which have not been used for many years but which are still in stock. This however does not apply to spare parts of machines which are still in use.

## Economic Order Quantity

In order to minimize the costs of placing the order and receiving the goods and keeping the items in stock the company needs to determine the quantity to be ordered at one time. This is usually determined based on a well - tested business model driven by the company's goals and the industry best practice.

## Work in Progress

Work in progress is the next component of inventory and is really the logical consequence of the fact that the process of manufacturing a product takes longer than one day. This is because at any point in time, there will be some units of a product which will still require some work to be done in order to turn them into finished products. As expected on some units, production work may have merely began while on others the work may have been advanced substantially and nearly completed. The company needs to manage the levels of its work in progress as part of its working capital and inventory management. The only way to reduce the quantum of work in progress at any point in time is to have proper production planning and control and to manage the production operations to ensure that work is not held up at any point longer than is absolutely necessary. In some cases, firms may deliberately keep a large quantity of work in progress so that when a special order is received from a customer requiring special features, the goods may be accordingly completed and delivered to the customer promptly.

**Finished Goods**

This is the third component of inventory. The function of finished goods inventory is two - fold. First, it helps avoid lost sales. Secondly it enables the company to have long production runs. Lost sales, called stock outs, means those sales which would have been made but for the fact that the goods demanded by the customer were not ready for delivery. Of course, if the customer is willing to wait, it is not a case of lost sale. The amount by which the company suffers because of lost sales is determined by the contribution of such sales, i.e. sales minus the variable expenses. With regards to production runs, it is obvious that if sales are fluctuating and if finished goods stock is kept at a fixed level only, production levels must be changed. This may become costly since it may mean idleness of machinery and labour or it may mean frequent retooling which is also costly. As far as retooling is concerned, there is an economic batch just as there is an economic order quantity. However there is another aspect of finished goods inventory and that is the interest etc. which is involved in maintaining inventories. Naturally, a company must balance the advantage from avoiding lost sales and having long production runs against the cost of keeping inventories. The company should have in place model for deriving the economic batch based on its goals and industry best practice.

**Techniques for Managing Inventory, Receivables and Payables**

The techniques that can be applied by a company to manage inventory, receivables and payables levels in the business are described below. As the working capital cycle usually starts with inventory we start with an exploration of the available techniques for reducing inventory or stock.

**Reducing Inventory**

For manufacturing or retail business companies, inventory is clearly an inevitable consequence of trading in products. Inventory can be in the form of raw materials, work in progress and finished goods ready for sale to customers. There can also be spare parts operations for business which are in the automotive industry like car manufacturers.

Businesses generally hold inventory stocks for the following reasons:

- As a buffer to manage uncertainty in supply such as lead times, quality and order fulfillment
- To purchase quantities that are economic
- To ensure continuous production runs with a complete set of components
- To stabilise manufacturing by using batch production
- To cope with unpredictable demand and the desire not to pass up a sales opportunity and
- To provide diversity and hence customer choice

In the wider working capital management strategy for the company the aim is to reduce inventory because it not only ties up cash in the business but also exposes the business to other financial costs, such as:

- **Storage**. This is the cost of warehouse space, warehouse staff and any particular storage conditions (such as chilled or secure storage)

- **Management**. The cost of management time in counting, finding, moving and inspecting

- **Obsolescence.** The risk that the product will become out of date and hence unsaleable if held for too long or because product enhancements are required to assure its usefulness.

- **Damage.** The inventory has the potential to become unsaleable as a result of breakage or damage.

- **Theft.** The pilferage or unauthorized removal of inventory from the stores or warehouse.

Inventory can be seen as a reservoir holding water. The "supply" of rain is unpredictable and therefore replenishment is unreliable. A large reservoir enables demand to be consistently met (apart from at times of extreme drought). If supply were more reliable the amount of water, or inventory that has to be held, could be reduced. Therefore to optimise the level of inventory is to increase certainty in both supply and demand.

The profile of inventory held by a company at any point in time can be said to be made up of four types of inventory depending on the level of inventory held. The four separate facets or types of inventory can be identified as

- **Pipeline inventory.** This is made up of inventory arriving in the storage of the company followed by sales, causing inventory to levels to slowly fall over subsequent days or weeks. When inventory levels are low a reorder takes place and the amount of inventory climbs back to a peak.

- **Safety inventory**. This is buffer inventory to ensure sales can continue with the uncertainties in demand and supply. The amount of uncertainty dictates the amount of safety inventory that needs to be held.

- **Lost revenue**. When inventory runs out this area represents the sales that could have been captured. Although specific unfulfilled orders can be identified and measured, the impact on long-term customer behaviour is more important as dissatisfaction can lead to customer accounts being closed. Managing and inquiring about lapsing accounts is an effective way of gathering feedback from defecting customers.

- **Excess inventory.** The needless holding of inventory that wastes resources in storage and may become obsolete.

From the foregoing it is clear that the central problem of inventory control is to reconcile the possible loss to the business that is likely to be experienced through interruption of production or loss of sales due to the failure to meet the customer's orders, on the one hand, and the cost of holding stocks large enough to provide the company with security against such loss, on the other. The models and techniques that have been devised in recent years to address the problem seek to quantify this delicate reconciliation that business must make.

**Reducing Pipeline Inventory**

To reduce pipeline inventory a business needs to make more frequent and smaller orders. Although this will reduce inventory levels it may push up supply costs, and the business may lose out on volume discounts and incur extra delivery charges.

To deal with the potential loss of volume discounts on orders, a call-off contract can be established, whereby an annual purchase volume is agreed with appropriate discounts and when inventory is required in the business it is called off for delivery. The benefit of this approach is achieving the prices of bulk buying combined with the convenience of small deliveries and low inventory levels. This type of deal is appropriate only for products or services where an annual level of demand can be predicted with certainty. There are also advantages for the supplier, which will have a confirmed order and will be able to produce the inventory at slack times.

As intimated above models and techniques have been devised to assist with the decision. One such well-established method is by calculating an economic order quantity (EOQ). Of course this model is a simplification of the very complicated situations which exist in factories and stores of any size. These inventory models are in effect abstractions from reality. However, they tend to preserve the central features of the inventory holding problems which confront modern business enterprises.

Usually the following inputs go into the model in determining the EOQ.

- Annual usage of an item
- Ordering cost (in total not per unit)
- Unit cost
- Holding cost per unit for one year

The economic quantity model or formula is used to set the reorder quantity (ROQ). But in some inventory management systems a reorder level (ROL) is also required. This is the amount of remaining inventory at which an order will be placed. There is a balance to be made between running the inventory too low with the risk of missing a sale through stock outs and being over cautious and ordering inventories too early thereby leading to excess inventory representing working capital tied up and not available for reinvestment or other uses.

In principle the strategy on economic order quantity will suggest that

- High-value items should be ordered often and low inventory levels should be maintained
- Low-value items of inventory should be ordered infrequently and higher levels of inventory maintained.

Although such models, and other more elaborate variants of them, can form the basis for quite effective inventory control systems, they need to be applied with care. This is due to the following salient factors:

- The models can, in some cases, lead to excessive investments in stocks since they take no account of the yield which might have been earned had money invested in inventory/stock been put to other use

- In some circumstances, unthinking application of the formula may give answers which theoretically correct but are in fact, not practicable

- It is not always practicable calculate EOQ for each of the many items which manufacturing and retail companies will have in their stores/ warehouses

- The lead time, which is the time between placing an order and receiving the goods, or materials is likely to vary, unless special arrangements have been made for regular periodic deliveries. One consequence of this is that the stocks used between placing an order and with suppliers and actually receiving a replenishment is not constant and that of a reorder level is established it must take account of this varying lead time.

- There is also the problem of varying rates of demand during the lead time. It is actually because of the need to deal with the problem of varying lead time and varying rate of demand that business decision makers use other statistical concepts of the mean and the standard deviation of the of the distributions of lead times and demands in determining the economic order quantity.

**Reducing Safety Inventory**

This is a combination of improved demand forecasting and supplier reliability. When these are worked through an inventory modelling tool, supplier reliability is normally shown to have the greatest impact on safety inventory, as explained below.

**Using Demand Forecasting to Manage Inventory**

Demand forecasting is the process of predicting future average sales on the basis of historical data samples and market intelligence. The volatility of demand from an average level is supplied from the safety inventory.

Any forecast is likely to be wrong, so the focus should be on understanding the range of potential forecast errors and the level of safety inventory that will cater for peak demand. An important additional calculation is forecast bias. This is the cumulative sum of under- or over-forecasting over a period of time. If, for example, the staff continually over-predict sales there will be a negative forecast bias, which will result in excess inventory and vice-versa.

A good process for demand forecasting involves collecting information as far down the supply chain as possible. For example, orders or bookings are better than sales when planning inventories and production. When forecasting the average demand it must be adapted for products with seasonal patterns - for example, garden products in summer and festive products for Christmas. The customer demand needs to be anticipated and a final date for reordering determined. Historic patterns of sales volumes can be a valuable source of reference for identifying appropriate inventory and ordering dates.

In the retail sector, the weather can play a large part in consumers' desire to go shopping and what they will buy. Care needs to be taken to manage inventory and potentially use sale or return as a way to reduce the risk of being left with inventory after the period of demand.

There are numerous forecasting packages available, all of which use combinations of mathematical models to simulate and predict future demand. The most common basic forecasting techniques are described below:

**Simple average**. In this forecasting technique the average of a selected range of past figures is used as the forecast for future periods. The more historical and past data that are selected, the more the fluctuations are dampened and the more accurate the forecast.

**Moving average.** The moving average approach involves taking the average of a specified number of past sales figures as the new forecast of future demand on a rolling basis.

**Exponential smoothing**. A weighting factor called alpha (a value between 0 and 1) is used to place a higher exponential bias on recent data and a lower exponential bias on older data. An alpha near 1 decays past data quickly (or weights current data more highly) and an alpha near 0 decays data more slowly (putting more emphasis on past data).

**Adaptive smoothing**. This is a forecasting technique where the weighting factor alpha is automatically selected based on the previous period's forecast error.

**Impact of Supplier Reliability on Safety Inventory**

Supplier reliability is very important in inventory management especially of safety inventory. There are two key factors that influence supplier reliability. These are the response time and quality of service/product provided. The more often a supplier is unreliable, the greater is the tendency for its customers to hold more safety inventory to compensate for supplier incompetence or likely delays in the fulfillment of orders placed. Thus, by changing suppliers or improving existing supplier reliability, a business can reduce its safety inventory levels in the knowledge that the supplier can be counted on to support the business efficiently through timely delivery and quality service.

The main variables that influence supplier reliability are discussed in more detail below:

**Importance of Supplier Response Time**

This is the lead time from the time a supplier receiving an order and being able to deliver it. Sourcing supplies from another continent to drive down cost may be advantageous at one level, but it is likely to extend lead time (for transportation) and require higher inventory levels to cover for uncertainty and potential delays. The risk of delays in supply can be passed back to the supplier in the form of guarantees and penalties, but the supplier providing the guarantee is likely to pass on the cost to the customer in its pricing, as it will with any fulfilment obligation imposed on it. The way to reduce response time and unit cost is to work with the supplier on how the necessary efficiencies can be achieved.

**Service and Product Quality**

Quality service and products can be driven by factors such as

- Supplier error through failures in fulfilling an order to specification
- Short or delayed delivery due to the inability to supply on time and in full, which is critical in supplier performance – in fact failure on this measure can be one of the biggest contributors to holding safety inventory
- Product quality resulting from delivery of supplies that are not fit for purpose, damaged, fail in service or not to specification required by the customer.

**Strategic Management of Supply Chain – Lean versus Agile**

The company needs to manage its relationship with its suppliers and by extension its inventory and stocks levels at each point in time in a strategic manner. This means the entire supply chain has to be strategically structured. In structuring a supply chain for sourcing of its supplies, it is important for the company to balance a supplier's ability to manage demand response times with reliability and split inventory requirements between supplies that need to be agile and those that can be lean. The differences between the two strategic objectives and the business implications are discussed briefly below:

> **Agile.** In striving for agility the primary goal of the company is revenue and growth. These are supplies where there is high volatility in demand and a quick response time to replenish the supplies is crucial. Thus agility is required businesses holding and selling highly fashionable clothing, where demand is unpredictable. Retailers need to be able to replenish the inventory of fashion clothing quickly should the product be popular, but they do not want to hold huge levels of inventory of such clothing in case demand is low. Agile typically means that products need to be manufactured near to the point of sale and therefore a short transport time is important.

> **Lean.** In pursuing leanness, as a strategy the primary goal of the business is cost reduction. Thus leanness is usually sought in situations where the demand for supplies in question is highly

predictable and therefore low-cost sourcing can be the primary focus of those charged with the management of the procurement process. A real life example can be seen in the basic clothing space involving items such as underwear, where retailers can be in a position to plan the required volumes of supplies with reasonable accuracy and inventory does not become obsolete. As volumes are predictable slow transport is not a problem.

**Managing the Portfolio of Inventory**

It is not unusual that as a manufacturing business grows it can develop an increasingly complex portfolio of products, variants, components, spares and sub-assemblies. The number of separate product items or stock-keeping units (SKUs) within the company's stock determines the range of inventory held. A variety of methods can be used by the company to reduce the value of this increasing investment in inventory. Each of these is discussed below:

**Reducing Inventory Volume through Simplification and Standardisation**

The volume of separate inventory items can be reduced by simplifying the range of products and components that are held. Some of the ways to achieve this are:

- Reducing the number of variants, such as sizes, colours, flavours or formats of products

- Standardising components where products share common parts - many of the car manufacturers use this approach; for example, Ford and General Motors use common parts across their range of brands
- Single sourcing to reduce the level of safety inventory and to make more frequent supplier deliveries economical.

**Reduction through Vendor-Managed Inventory**

Another inventory reduction method that can be adopted by a company is to use vendor-managed inventory (vmi) which is a process where a supplier will retain ownership of inventory and manage its provision within a customer's site. A good example of vendor-managed inventory is greetings cards in supermarkets. There are numerous types of cards, slow rates of stock turnover and complexity in coordinating the replenishment of shelves. As result, many supermarkets have entered into vmi arrangements with their suppliers: the supplier is responsible for shelf filling and the supermarket does not buy the product until a customer purchases it. The benefit of this approach for the supermarket is that there is neither investment in inventory nor disposal of unpopular or seasonal styles that remain unsold.

The same approach can be applied in manufacturing where contracts with suppliers can be structured for the provision of components straight into line-side storage areas. The management of lead times and safety inventory remains with the supplier. Penalties can be built in whereby a supplier is "fined" when a component has run out and continuous manufacturing is prevented.

**Inventory Management on a Sale or Return basis**

A third approach of inventory reduction is usually applied where there is uncertainty about the use or sale of a product and hence the risk can be left with the supplier, with inventory being taken into a business on a sale-or-return basis. If the product is used it is paid for, and if it is not used it is simply sent back to the supplier. This involves no risk or inventory for the company and is an efficient way for the company to try out new product ideas and suppliers, to determine which one will likely be a winner. However, because unit costs may be higher under such an arrangement, once volume levels are established it may make sense to revert to an outright purchase model.

**Ensuring the Supply Model of the Business is fit for Purpose**

Every business model that drives its philosophy regarding how it manages it business including how it supplies goods and services to its customers. The latter is usually referred to as the company's supply model. A company can use a range of supply models to decouple supply and demand within its business and supply relationships. A supply model determines the point at which components are assembled into a finished product, committing a manufacturer to one variant of its product portfolio. For example, a car manufacturer that builds cars in advance of receiving a customer order needs to pre-select attributes such as paint colour and interior fabric. If the combination proves unpopular, the variant will remain in inventory a long time. However, if the car is painted and trimmed after an order is placed, there will be no need for inventory to be held and far more colour options can be offered. The disadvantage of this approach is the time delay between an order being placed and the finished product being delivered. In general we can distinguish between five types of supply models as discussed below depending on how the customer's order is fulfilled and the different inventory issues that each of these supply models raise or which drive the application of the model.

**Assemble to order**. This supply model is based on the act that the product can be highly tailored to the specific customer requirements, each of which may be unique, enabling a wide range of options and choices to be offered to the customer. An example of a company that uses this supply model is Dell Computers which prides itself in enabling computers to be built to customer order from sub-assemblies.

**Make to order**. This supply model is very similar to the one above except that in this case the fulfilment of the customer's order or demand is through the provision of a highly personalized product or service enabling a wide range of options and choices to be availed to the customer with minimal waste realized by the company from preempting customer selection, which like in the case above, is likely to be different, in each case or order. This model is used by restaurants where meals are made based ion the customer's order from pre-purchased raw food ingredients.

**Sell from Inventory**. This supply model is common with retailers with lots of stores branches and outlets and is driven by the fact that a limited range of inventory can be held or stocked with the volume of demand in each location likely being different thereby requiring high levels of safety inventory the same level of volumes.

**Source and then Make to Order**. This supply model is applicable, where the product required by the customer takes a long time to design and source before production can be started in order to fulfil the order. This usually involves very highly individualized products without any obsolescent inventory. A good real life example of suppliers who use this model are ship builders and airplane manufacturers where the components and raw materials required to make the product are purchased after an order has been received from the customer. Operationally "source and make to order" together with the "assemble to order" models tend to have a very slow response time with inventory levels being order - driven and maintained at very low levels with variations in the product supplies being very many.

**Deliver from Inventory**. This fifth supply model obtains in cases where delay in the distribution and fulfillment of the customer's need is permissible and where demand is more predictable requiring lower levels of safety inventory to be kept by the company. Also greater range of products can be offered to customers. An example of a business that uses this model is Amazon, across the whole range of their goods with centralized distribution points set up in different locations. Like in the case of sell from inventory operationally this model has a very fast response time, the inventory levels which are usually forecast driven being maintained at a high level with very limited product variations.

Much of the advantage of "fulfil and deliver from inventory" can be gained by those that "fulfil and sell from inventory" by using central warehouses that frequently deliver to the outlets. This enables each outlet to maintain low levels of safety inventory. As shown from the descriptions of the supply models above each model has operational advantages and disadvantages. A key lesson from the foregoing is that there is no ideal position in terms of supply model. Depending on the nature of the business and customer requirements the optimum decoupling point can be identified by the company and applied.

**The Role of Distributors in the Management of Inventory Levels**

For businesses that have a large portfolio of products and a wide and diverse customer base, a viable route to market is to use distributors to manage the inventory and the high-volume, low-value transactions. An example is multinational company, Unilever. The company distributes directly to major retailers, but small owner-manager shops have to source Unilever products through a wholesaler. This means that Unilever delivers whole pallets of products to a few large customers- that is the large retailers and the wholesalers who constitute the backbone of Unilever's distribution system. The distributors and wholesalers break the pallets down into individual cartons and products to sell in smaller units. For Unilever, there are substantial cost savings in handing over high-volume, low-value transactions for others to distribute. This is the principle of the Pareto analysis or the 80/20 rule, which suggests that 80% of revenue is derived from 20% of customers and vice versa. The percentages may not be precise, but there is empirical evidence to demonstrate that indeed a substantial part of any organisation's infrastructure is set up to service a large group of small value customers from which little profit is derived.

The use of distributors is not only beneficial for large multinationals like Unilever. The distributors themselves also have a vested interest in the way the supply and distribution chain is structured. The advantage to the distributors is that they can consolidate the portfolio of products and goods from a number of manufacturers (like Coca-cola, Nestle, Procter & Gamble, Cadburys, Kraft foods, and so on) and derive higher value per customer than they would be able to achieve from dealing with a single manufacturer.

CHAPTER SIX

STRATEGIC MANAGEMENT OF RECEIVABLES AND
DEBTORS

**Accounts Receivable and Management of Credit**

In order to encourage sales it is a normal business practice these days for companies to extend credit to their customers. A company which insists only on cash sales could soon find that the sales it is making are not adequate to assure a sufficient level of profitability. However, selling to customers on credit always has the risk that the debtor may not pay outright leading to bad debts, or may pay late denying the company the use of these resources in alternative investments. As a matter of good business sense a company has to decide for itself as to how much risk in respect of bad debts or delayed payments it is willing to take. In the light of this the company must try to frame rules that it can apply for ascertaining the credit worthiness of people or other companies, usually called counterparties, who would like to have credit extended to them without much risk. One of the most vital recent developments in the credit granting space, in our modern world today, is the emergence of special credit rating agencies which assess the credit worthiness of people and companies and provide credit ratings which helps lenders or those wishing to extend trade credit to assess the level of credit risk of a potential customer. Previously, it was the opinion of bankers and other firms which guided a company in extending credit to its customers. Other than the credit rating of the customer, another important and relevant consideration is the company's previous dealings with the customer.

The key issues to consider when deciding whether or not to extend credit to a customer are:

- o The company or the individuals present financial position as shown by its balance sheet
- o The scale of the customer's operations and efficiency with which the operations of the company or individual are being carried out
- o The customers character as to trustworthiness or otherwise.

Any person who is seeking credit should not only have the willingness to pay the debt but also the capacity to do so. The capacity comes really from the person's ability to sell the goods which he buys on credit, for example, collect the cash, if he has also sold it on credit and use the proceeds to clear its debt. Therefore, the scale of the customer's operations, or his turnover, and his profitability are very important considerations and factors in assessing whether to extend credit to the customer. It is very easy, if a company adopts an overly liberal credit policy, to make a customer bankrupt by merely extending too much credit to him causing him to buy so much goods on credit that he is not able to in turn sell and use the proceeds therefrom to pay up his debts.

It is important for the company to strike a balance in its decisions with respect to extending credit to customers. A company can be too conservative or too adventurous or liberal with respect to its credit policies and rules. A good indication of where the company stands in terms of this balance can be determined from the ratio of its bad debts to its sales. If the company has no bad debts then the implication is that the credit policy is clearly two conservative and the company could gain by liberalizing its credit policy just a little bit, opening an opportunity for more sales to be made by the company thereby generating or earning higher profits in the process. On the other hand, if the level of its bad debts are too much or too high, then it is likely that the company's credit policy is too lax and liberal meaning that the company could benefit from some additional tightening of its credit policy with, possibly, the introduction of stricter rules for granting credit and by putting tougher procedures in place for collecting the receivables more strictly and quickly. From a strategic standpoint, the main point to note, though, is that extending credit to customers should be looked upon by the company as a dynamic sales technique rather than a mere accommodation of customers' wishes

## Guidelines for Effective Receivables Management

In order to ensure that its receivables and debtors are well and optimally managed world class companies usually apply the following guidelines:

- They have the right mental attitude to the control of credit and make sure that the customer gets the priority it deserves and that the credit and the cash collection are well managed.
- Establish clear credit practices as a matter of company policy which are rigorously applied.

- Make sure that the adopted credit practices are clearly understood by staff, suppliers and customers and that staff are properly trained in their application.

- They are always professional when accepting new customer accounts, and especially larger ones.

- Check out each customer's credit thoroughly before they offer credit. Use credit rating agencies, bank references, industry sources etc. Continuously review these limits when you suspect tough times are coming or if operating in a volatile   sector

- Keep very close to the larger customers and ensures timely follow – up and diagnosis of payments and collections issues

- Invoice the customers promptly and clearly to avoid errors and delays

- They consider charging penalties on overdue accounts to encourage prompt payment

- Consider accepting credit /debit cards as a payment option to accelerate cash inflows

- Monitor their debtor balances and ageing schedules very closely, and don't let any debts get too large or too old thereby making them too difficult to collect.

- Establish credit limits for each customer... and ensure all staff stick to them.

**Reducing Receivables**

In the business-to-business market customers expect to purchase on credit; inevitably, this will delay the receipt of cash from one to three or more months from the date of sale. In the consumer market cash sales are more common. Credit-card settlement, although similar to speed of payment, carries a cost as credit-card companies charge a fee for handling the transaction which is equivalent to an interest payment for credit plus administration.

The credit terms that a business offers can be an intrinsic part of the overall customer proposition; for example, furniture companies that offer interest-free credit for a year or car companies that provide extended credit over three years. These kinds of credit terms aid sales but have a cost, which needs to be recognised, and a cash flow effect, which the business will need to fund.

Accelerating cash collection may not always be optimal for the overall business model and therefore only actions that are consistent with the business model should be considered. All sales on credit involves the risk of bad debt from non-payment through companies becoming insolvent. Even where purchases are settled using credit cards there is still a risk due to credit-card fraud or even forged notes. It is therefore critical for companies selling on credit to ensure that proper care is taken in validating the counterparty with whom business is being carried out and the means of settlement so as to reduce such losses to the extent possible as it is not feasible to eliminate such risks entirely.

**Credit checks**

Before advancing credit facilities to customers, to allow purchases on account, it is important to check that the prospective customers are bona fide and able to pay. Typically, this would be achieved through undertaking a credit check and perhaps requesting and obtaining a bank reference on the potential counterparty or customer. Although these procedures do not always guarantee payment, but they will go a long way in preventing dealings with high-risk customers. A credit check completed by one of the credit rating agencies will usually involve an analysis of the customer's accounts and will be similar to the financial ratio analysis. The areas of focus in a credit check will usually include:

- Evidence of a sustainable and profitable business
- Leverage – i.e. debt to equity ratio of under fifty percent (50%)
- Track record of the counterparty's payment history
- Tangible networth - the surplus of uncharged assets available to creditors
- Relative performance of the business compared to others in its industry sector
- Details of court judgments against the business
- Details of existing mortgages and charges taken by other lenders over the assets of the business

- Details of directors and their other directorships.

From this information the credit rating agency will form its view on the counterparty's financial strength, risk and maximum credit limit. Using a credit reference a business can, based on the credit ratings, create its own credit limit for each of the counterparties with whom it wishes to do business. The amount will typically start low and increase with good payment experience. Once a credit limit is in place it is important to have procedures to prevent a customer from exceeding the limit. This is achieved by careful monitoring of the account and either suspending additional sales until the account has been reduced by a cash payment or by increasing the limit in line with good credit history.

**Customer Account Management**

Business organizations, as matter of good business practice have a client account management system in place although how these systems operate may differ in their scope and function depending on the nature of the company's business and the industry within which it is operating. As part of best practice customer account management, when a large trading or manufacturing organization receives an invoice from a supplier there is usually a well-defined procedure for validation and payment of the invoice. Smaller organizations will normally have similar systems, but they may not be as sophisticated. If an invoice which does not comply with these validation systems is received the system will automatically trigger a rejection of the invoice and a delay in payment ensue while the invoice is returned and corrected. Understanding a customer's invoice processing system is a simple way to ensure that there are as few barriers as possible to prompt payment of the invoice.

Some of the common reasons a customer's invoices may be rejected by the Accounts Payable Department, include, for example:

- **Lack of Purchase order numbers.** Many systems require a purchase order to be raised before any goods or services are accepted as part of good internal control over purchases. It is therefore expected that a valid invoice should to state the purchase order number in order for it to be validated and approved for payment. The basis for the purchase order will be either a contract or a specific quote that has been provided by the supplier.

- **Incorrect information.** This may sound obvious, but it is a common cause of invoice rejection. Common errors include incorrect quantity (particularly if there was a short delivery), price not matching what was agreed in the contract, discount terms not agreeing to what is indicated in the contract.

- **Incorrect address.** Centralisation of organisations has meant that transactional accounting may be based at a different site or even in a different country from where the product or service was delivered. It is therefore important that the address is correct as it is one of the control variables included in modern payment systems to ascertain validity of the invoice.

An important action that a company should take to reduce or avoid having an invoice rejected is to make sure that the relevant staff working on raising and preparation of invoices avoid making mistakes and that if they do they do not the same mistake again. This can be achieved by ensuring there is proper training and procedures manual in place which staff especially, the new staff, can refer to. The role of those charged with the supervision of the relevant staff involved in the preparation of the invoices should be as much about correcting the errors as about putting processes in place to avoid it being repeated.

## Using Ageing Schedule or Debt Report

Most companies have implemented accounting systems which are able to produce an aged debt report, usually called ageing schedule, which will analyse all the unpaid invoices by the date they should have been paid and highlights the unpaid invoices or debtors according to the age or length of time of the outstanding debtors or receivables. On the basis of this aging schedule, payment of overdue invoices re usually rigorously chased based on some set of strict rules stating the required sanctions to be applied while an invoice remains unpaid. Some of the rules and sanctions usually applied are follows:

- Once an invoice is over 60 days old (overdue for payment), further sales should be suspended until the arrears are cleared;
- Enforcement notices should commence after 90 days and
- Legal proceedings started to recover the cash after 120 days.

A disciplined approach for dealing with credit sales and overdue invoices that is well understood by customers and the accounts receivable staff helps to focus attention on the issue and encourage payment ahead of others that are less forceful. Getting and bringing cash in on time from its receivables is one of the most important controls for any business especially if it which wishes to keep its bad debts down.

Enforcement of late payment sanctions needs to take into account the dynamics of how the payment system works in practice. Many accounting systems will report the status of customers' accounts at the end of the month, which may not be necessarily representative of the payment system they adopt. For example, many businesses pay their suppliers on the last trading day of the month which means the cash is received in the first few days of the next month. Therefore a customer account may look over the limit at the end of the month but may subsequently be regularised a few days later. To manage the effect of this common practice, enforcement action should only be taken once a proper reconciliation of the customers' account has been rigorously undertaken and all cash sent in by the customer in the previous month has been received (potentially the third working day of the month).

Having a very rigorous receivables collection and sanctions process may not please customers, but it should be balanced against the risk of a bad debt. In a business transaction there are of course good and bad customers. The bad customers are those that demand considerable attention and do not pay their invoices, unless they are followed up. A business may be more successful by choosing not to deal with them and focusing on the good customers that are easy to serve and who pay their invoices on time.

**The Role of the Business Model in Receivables Management**

There is always a business model underpinning how a company handles its sales and dealings with customers whether or not this is explicitly stated. Even when this is not explicit it is apparent from their business behavior in dealing with debtors of receivables. This business model ultimately drives the level of receivables or debtors in the company's books at any point in time. This means that a change in the business model can impact a company's receivables - either upwards or downwards. It may be possible to reduce the volume of, or avoid having, receivables by changing the business model as mobile phone companies have done with "pay-as-you-go" services.

With the advent of mobile telephony, mobile phone companies' original business model was to have account customers who paid for their phone invoices once in a month in arrears. This meant that they received the mobile phone services and paid for it later - a month later thereby tying cash resources. For low-user customers the cost of issuing invoices, collecting and even chasing small amounts was more expensive than the amounts involved. The mobile phone companies therefore decided to introduce the prepayment service, using prepaid smart cards, where the mobile phone company receives the cash in advance of the usage and the low-user customers spend their advance as they use the service. With the prepayment approach there is no bad debt risk, for the companies as there are no receivables, and there is the benefit of receiving cash in advance. There is also an additional benefit for the mobile companies, since some prepaid cards also have a time limit built in so that a proportion of prepaid cards will have a value that expires without any service being provided. Clearly, this shows that changing the business model can be a way to reduce receivables by achieving an accelerated profile of cash receipts and a reduction in credit risk to the business.

**Prompt Payment Discount**

We have discussed the role of prompt payment discount in the management of a company's accounts payable - dealings with its creditors. It can also applied in the opposite direction in the management of the companies receivables- dealings with the company's debtors. Putting a prompt payment discount is a viable way to accelerate the receipt of cash by providing the customer/debtor an incentive, usually a discount that is well worth the customer accepting: Prompt payment discounts ranging from 1.5% to 2% on the invoice amount are quite common for payments made within 30 days. However, this process has to be carefully managed as some intransigent customers will not only take the discount but also not pay promptly and continue to pay late beyond the thirty days credit period provided.

statement thereby making them more fun and encouraging children to make their parents open the invoice.

**Guaranteeing Payments**

When businesses go international and trade across their country of domicile borders the ability to collect cash becomes more difficult. In such cross border trades, there are potentially two legal systems operating and pursuing the customer for payment or nonpayment can be expensive. Therefore a letter of credit (LOC) is used to provide a payment contract for goods or services. The LOC is an irrevocable payment undertaking drawn up by the customer's bank that binds the bank to pay a fixed sum of money to another party on fulfilment of certain criteria (the delivery of goods). The credit risk is therefore with the customer's bank and not the customer itself.

There is also the potential for government support with international trade as governments are always keen to promote exports. In this regard, some governments will operate credit guarantee schemes which act much like insurance. For a small payment the debt can be guaranteed and on occurrence of various specified conditions the agency will pay the debt and assume responsibility for its collection.

**Automating Settlement through Direct Debit Settlement**

For consumers making frequent payments, typically for services or utilities, a way to take control of their settlement is to ask them to pay by direct debit. This is the process where the supplier is authorised to initiate withdrawals from consumers' bank accounts. Where this mode of payment is applied, there are strict controls on this and in most developed economies, depending on the local regulations, it enables funds to be withdrawn 14 days after advice of the amount to be taken. Although consumers need to have cash in their bank account for this to work, it is a highly efficient way to automate settlement and reduce administration costs.

**Using Vendor Finance Programme**

The credit terms offered to customers can be a significant part of the overall value proposition. This is particularly important for selling high-price consumer goods. The offer of extended credit with low-interest or even interest-free finance is common. The manufacturers or retailers offering these deals may not want to carry the cost of funding this credit and will therefore set up an arrangement with a bank, which takes on the debt and collects it in the same way as it would any normal loan. The incentive for the bank is that it will pay the retailer less than the amount it collects. For example, if a piece of furniture is on sale for USD 1,000 with interest-free credit, the bank will give the retailer, say, USD 900 and take the difference of USD 100 to cover the cost of interest until cash is received from the customer. These finance packages can be branded so the customer does not know the financial institution behind the transaction.

**Funding Construction Projects**

Many businesses invoice customers on completion of services or delivery of products. For businesses involved in construction projects, where there will be significant investments in raw materials and work in progress, a substantial amount of working capital can be committed. To offset this investment it is important to have a schedule of "payments on account" which match the investment or even provide a cash positive position. To satisfy customers that they are paying for genuine work that has been completed, it is normal to have the work in progress "certified" by an independent expert. The advance payments need not be limited to just the costs incurred to date; they can also include a proportion of the profit that will arise on the whole transaction.

# CHAPTER SEVEN

## STRATEGIC MANAGEMENT OF ACCOUNTS PAYABLE/ CREDITORS

A company's strategic approach to the management of its accounts payable processing affects two important strategic business matters: cash flow and supplier relationships. Applying best practices in the management of accounts payable ensures that the process both contributes positively to cash flow and supports mutually beneficial relationships with suppliers.

With respect to cash flow, applying accounts payable processing best practices makes a significant difference both in minimizing late-payment costs - such as late-payment penalties, interest charges, and lost prompt-payment discounts - and in creating efficient accounts payable and business operations. In general, a company with smooth-running, streamlined accounts payable operations saves money by processing invoices with a minimum of staff and a low cost of materials.

Regarding supplier relations and promotion of mutually beneficial relationships with suppliers, company management needs to be aware that its actions in the accounts payable space inevitably impact the trust between the company and its suppliers. Whether or not the company honors its agreed-upon payment terms - by paying its invoices on time, as promised - does more to build trust with its suppliers or to tear it down than any other action the company can take. From a strategic standpoint, strong relations with suppliers is important to the company because suppliers provide valuable trade credit, have ideas for new methods and products, and can play an important role in customer service.

**Goals of Strategic Approach to Accounts Payables Management**

The application of accounts payable best practices in a strategic manner can facilitate the achievement of the following three goals:

- To pay invoices on a predetermined schedule of the company's choosing,
- To ensure the accuracy and authenticity of invoices that the company pays, and
- To process accounts payable paperwork with a minimum of handling and expense.

**Deferring Settlement of Payables**

An important part of optimizing working capital is to defer the settlement of accounts payable. This might be the easiest of the three areas to control because a business has the ability to dictate when payables are to be settled, but there are implications regarding the relationship this creates with suppliers and the impact on the overall reputation and image of the business. An abuse of credit terms will jeopardise the willingness of suppliers to continue supplying goods to the company or motivate the suppliers to offer sub-optimal prices in an attempt to cover the cost of the credit provided.

The actions of a business that is trying to defer payment are in direct contradiction to a supplier that is trying to apply the principles of reducing its receivables. A contractual agreement is needed that is accepted by both parties and complied with for all payments. Without such agreement relationships are likely to become strained as each party pushes its preferred position. The attitude of suppliers at times of urgent need by the company will be crucial, particularly if products are required at short notice or to a certain specification in order to fulfill an order.

**Strategic Management of Supply Agreements**

It is important that the company approaches the management of its accounts payable portfolio and the entire relationship with suppliers in a strategic manner. So it needs to be aware of when it is most likely to get more favourable terms from the supplier and take maximum advantage of it – in working capital management terms we call it "leveraging the relationship with the supplier".

In setting up supply agreements the easiest time to agree and obtain favourable payment terms is when a supplier has the opportunity to win a new contract. At such moments the supplier will be hungry for the business and may be more amenable to negotiating the quoted prices downwards and willing to offer soft payment and pricing terms as it seeks to conclude the supply agreement. Once the supplier is in place and the business's dependency on it grows, the supplier's position is usually much stronger and better payment and other terms will be much more difficult to renegotiate.

One of the most common terms for settlement is to pay at the end of the month following the month of invoice. Therefore any products or services purchased in, say, the month of June, may be required to be settled at the end of July, for example. Once terms have been agreed it is important that they should be complied with to avoid damaging the long-term supplier-buyer relationship.

However, if a business is on the typical terms mentioned above the most advantageous time to purchase products or services is at the beginning of a month as payment will not be required for 60 days, compared with purchases at the end of the month that will need to be paid for after only a shorter period, say thirty (30) days.

**Evaluating Incentives Offered by Suppliers**

It is common for suppliers to offer buyers incentives in order to drive up their sales. These sometimes include discounts for volumes. Suppliers keen to see their order books grow may offer volume-based discounts that are justifiable through the economies of scale that result from large orders. And of course buyers need to evaluate the benefits of the incentives against their own business objectives.

Some of the more common types of discounts offered by suppliers include and or are based on:

- **Order size**. The larger the size of order the higher the discount offered. The rationale is that placing large orders ensures the supplier is able to fulfill them with long and efficient production runs.

- **Delivery discount.** The number and frequency of delivery is also critical. Suppliers always prefer having one bulk delivery rather than several small deliveries as it enables efficiencies to be achieved in the management of the related logistics. Thus suppliers encourage clients to make bulk orders which are delivered in bulk by offering bulk delivery discounts.

- **Overrides.** This involves extending annual discounts to customers based on total purchasing during a year. Suppliers will often set these at levels above the previous year's volume to encourage growth. The temptation is to place a large order at the end of the year to hit the override discount. This will create high inventory and is likely to prevent the following year from reaching the volume where the override discount takes effect.

In managing accounts payables it is important for the company to secure a low unit cost in sourcing of its supplies and should not approach the incentives offered blindly. Bulk purchasing creates inventory and accelerates payables, but it may be more cost effective overall.

**Evaluating Prompt Payment Incentives**

It is also common for suppliers to offer prompt-payment discounts to customers in order to improve their cash liquidity position and drive their receivables down. As noted above, the company who are the customer in this case, must approach the incentives offered in in this regard in a strategic manner rather than just take it at face value. This is because prompt payment of accounts payable is not necessarily costless. Therefore the cost of funding the accelerated payment needs to be balanced against the value of the discount achieved. One way is to compare the benefit of the prompt - payment discount with the company's weighted average cost of capital (WACC). In general, if the company's WACC is, say twelve percent (12%), then the prompt-payment discount needs to be more than 1% per month to be worth accepting.

From a strategic standpoint the company should seek to optimise the cost and cash flow benefit from suppliers. To this end it is important for company management to ensure that the performance measurement metrics are strategic and set to incentivize the appropriate behavior for purchasing departments. If for example, the performance metric for a department is set to measure cost reduction, its staff will likely be tempted to give away accounts payment efficiencies in order to secure higher discounts. For this reason, the performance measures need to be set to encourage a balanced response that minimizes the total supply cost to the business. That is there is need to look at the total cost to the business rather than the cost of the purchase made or price paid for it in isolation.

**Changing the Business Model for Accounts Receivables**

It is important to understand the business model of the company and how this drives its growth in inventory levels and cash flows of the business. One way that companies use to avoid holding excess inventory and to defer accounts payables is to delay the purchase of products from a supplier until they are actually required in the business. For example, in a manufacturing business where there is a regular supply contract in place, it is likely that both the business and supplier will hold a buffer of inventory. The business will hold inventory to meet volatility in demand or delays in supply. The supplier will hold inventory to meet volatility in demand and to fulfil orders at short notice. By the two parties combining their inventory in one location, in a strategic partnership, both are able to reduce inventory and only hold one buffer to meet all demands - i.e. demand from both sides. In practice, this involves the business providing the supplier with space to store the inventory and the purchase of inventory takes place as it is used in the business. As discussed in the section on reducing inventory, there are of course, several ways of doing this.

In the current world of integrated information technology, the inventory management and accounts payables system can be further enhanced to include automated billing. This is possible because as products are made the number of components in each finished item is known, real time. Therefore computer systems can identify the number of items that have been purchased from the supplier and using an automated price list an equally automated invoice can be generated. The resulting invoice can then be settled based on the agreed terms.

If well managed, this whole process becomes highly efficient in terms of enabling the company to achieve both process and operational efficiencies: fewer inventory counts, automated invoicing, a lack of invoice errors and automated settlement all of which contribute to the efficient management of the company's working capital.

CHAPTER EIGHT

STRATEGIC MANAGEMENT OF CASH

Strategic cash management can be defined as constituting all the activities taken by the company management to ensure the effective planning, monitoring, control and management of cash, liquid and near liquid resources at the company's disposal so as to ensure that there is adequate cash available to meet the company's commitments at each point in time and in the most cost - effective manner. Cash management also involves the forecasting, control and stewardship of the company's financial assets and safeguarding them from fraud, error or loss. These critical cash management activities revolve around, but are not limited to, day-to-day cash control, cash held at the bank, cash receipts, cash or cheque payments and short term investments and borrowings. Thus cash management is a critical component of a company's liquidity management, without which serious operational difficulties would ensue.

**The Need for a Cash Balance**

Cash is a very vital component of working capital. A company requires a healthy cash balance for three primary business purposes:

- **Day to day expenses**. A company needs to meet the day to day expenses it incurs, if current receipts for any reason fall short of the current payments that the company needs to make then it will have to use its cash balance to meet its obligations. Normally, it is expected that the proceeds from the sale of goods and realizations from the company's receivables and short term debts would enable the company to not only pay for its current liabilities on time but also enable it to make payments for the expenses as and when they occur.

- **Profitable opportunity**. Once in a lifetime opportunities for the company to make profits may occur when they are least expected. So a company needs to have sufficient cash balance in its coffers to be able to take advantage of any profitable opportunity that may present itself and which may not wait if there is no ready cash available immediately to leverage it - i.e. profit from it. This is the reason that many forward looking companies maintain idle cash balances so that, if an opportunity for acquiring a good company, which is perhaps undervalued in the market, arises, the company can avail itself of the opportunity promptly and immediately before its competitors or before the opportunity is lost.

- **Safety margin.** Unbelievable as it may sound, the mantra of "safety first" also does apply to business enterprises, too. Companies that are successful always make sure that they keep a safety margin in terms of liquid cash at hand so that if an emergency should develop, there will be ready cash to meet the emergency. This need for a safety net, may be said to lend credence to the old saying that a man has only three friends - an old dog, an old wife and cash at bank - may be not necessarily in the order of importance. A company cannot have the first two categories of friends, unless of course it is a sole entrepreneur, hence it will definitely need a good and healthy cash balance at bank.

The amount of cash that a company may require to be able to meet its day to day expenses can be estimated by careful cash budgets. However, in order to determine how much cash the company needs to maintain to be able to take advantage of unexpected profit opportunities and or take care of unforeseen emergencies, each company has to decide based on their past experience or some established decision criteria. However, it cannot be a case of one size fits all! However, as noted earlier, the company needs to ensure that it strikes an optimal balance in terms of the level of cash it maintains because idle cash is as wasteful as idle machinery and lack of cash is in itself also likely to be very dangerous for the company.

When firms speak of shortage of working capital they in fact often possibly imply scarcity of cash resources.

The functions of cash management include the following activities, which normally fall under treasury operations in some organisations;

- **Forecasting:** The accurate forecasting of the company's cash needs including the timing and amount of cash flows
- **Control:** This has to do with controlling or validating disbursements to ensure that they are consistent with the

financial regulations and duly approved before settlement speeding collections of cash

- **Safeguarding**. This involves protection of the company's cash resources from fraud, error and loss.

- **Funding**. This aspect of cash management has to do with arranging the necessary funding to cover temporary and longer term cash short-falls.

- **Investing**. In this regard cash management is focused on ensuring that excess cash is invested while at the same time ensuring risk is minimized, return is maximized and liquidity is assured.

**Cash Forecasting**

Accurate cash forecasting and liquidity management are critical treasury functions in any organization.

Cash management in effect starts with the accurate forecasting of present and future cash flows. This is important because numerous financial and business decisions are based on the forecast including how to manage current and future cash balances.

The format and level of detail included in a cash forecast depends on two factors. The user and the use to which he wishes to put the forecast data. Thus, the level of detailed data required by a manager will differ from that required by, say a trader, who is responsible for investment of excess cash. Another factor that determines the structure of the forecast is the technology used to build the forecast. For example, the use of database, as opposed to a spreadsheet could provide additional flexibility in terms of the details provided and the level of drill down that can be undertaken by the user of the forecast. In practice forecasts built around databases is more amenable to reformatting and analysis for different user. The important thing is to ensure that the data provided in the forecast is appropriate to the needs of the user.

**Forecasting Methods**

There are several methods that can be used to build forecasts. Most forecasting methods tend to revolve either around the use of formal approaches of forecasting involving historical data and statistical analysis or are based on the experience and knowledge of the individual doing the forecasting. A major pitfall of the non - formal approach of forecasting is that it does not provide a backup should the employee with the necessary expertise leave the organization or the particular unit.

Many organizations apply the following approaches is cash forecasting:

- **Scheduling.** This is usually the simplest approach of forecasting. It involves scheduling a large-value or discrete cash inflows or outflows representing cash flows that will either occur or not occur. Scheduling tends to be used for cash flows that are material to the organization.

- **Distribution.** This method of forecasting is used where an amount is likely to occur the amount is not known with certainty. For example, cheque clearings, or trade receivables. Distribution is used for forecasted amounts that consist of a number of items which taken together may be material but individually not material nor easy to forecast with accuracy. Once major cash flows have been scheduled, the distribution cash be used to forecast the approximate amounts of cash flows. In tracking historical cash flows it is important to take into account seasonal variations and to adjust for the changes in the company's business or cash flows

- **Statistical Analysis.** This involves the use of simple regression which attempt to create a formula that explains the causal relationship between a particular occurrence (independent variable) and the resultant cash flows which are considered the dependent variables. Where several factors are involved multiple regression analysis would be applied to model them.

Simple and multiple regression analysis can be done quickly in a spreadsheet or in specialized financial software. However close attention needs to be to be paid to the data used, it limitations and the validity of the presumed causal relationship.

- **Reconciliation**. Reconciliation involves the comparison of the transactions that were expected to happen and those that actually happened. A reconciliation adjusts for the items that differ from the forecast both those that have unexpectedly cleared the account and those that have unexpectedly not cleared the account. Reconciliations is a highly automated process in many organizations through treasury software, electronic and transaction services. It is important that automated reconciliation processes provide for adequate matching to ensure that fraudulent transaction do not pass through the reconciliation system. Experience shows that where the matching is only based on amounts, items where the payee has been fraudulently changed may not be flagged.

**Other Disbursement Methods**

Other methods for disbursements that many companies use in managing their cash resources include the setting up of imprest accounts that are funded periodically at a particular balance for a specific purpose, multiple drawee checks that can he presented at a bank other than the bank on which they are drawn, and payable-through drafts that are drawn on the payer rather than the payer's bank. It is noteworthy that Debit cards and credit cards have become increasingly popular methods of payment. It is difficult think of any sizeable company who are not otherwise using any of the above techniques for their managing cash flows.

Corporate Purchasing cards is another payment innovation introduced recently which involves issuing company staff with a credit card for use in some purchases relevant to the company and helps companies reduce the cost of purchasing for small items and amounts. There is significant cost associated with purchasing small items using purchase orders, receiving, and invoicing. Corporate purchase cards, which should have systems in place to reduce opportunities for misuse, cost a fraction of the purchase order method.

**Cash Aggregation**

Cash aggregation is the collection and utilization of cash as quickly as possible. Depending on the financial institution and the country in which an organization operates, cash aggregation services can assist in managing dispersed cash pools for use at a central location. This may help to improve returns on excess cash balances or make cash available for debt reduction.

Organizations that operate branch and subsidiary operations may find that each requires one or more bank accounts.

Typically, there is a need for funds in those accounts, even if the amounts are small, to cover unexpected payments or requirements. Organizations with many operations and bank accounts may find that significant funds are tied up in these balances and could he better utilized through centralization. Cash aggregation services may simplify account administration and control. Although there are others, some of the most common tools to assist with cash aggregation include zero-balance accounts, controlled disbursement accounts, and pooling.

**Use of Zero-Balance Account**

A zero-balance account (ZBA) automatically moves funds from individual accounts within the same financial institution to a master concentration account on a regular, typically daily, basis. While the individual accounts may be used for cash collection or disbursements (e.g., payroll), the master concentration account is used to collect and utilize excess funds from the individual accounts within the structure.

The ZBA is a disbursement account on which checks can be written. As checks are cleared against the account, an automated transfer of funds occurs from the master account to cover them. With zero balancing, individual positive account balances arc reduced to zero (or to another predetermined balance), while accounts in deficit are increased to zero or other balance. Funds transfers actually occur, and as a result there are legal and tax considerations de-pending on the corporate or organizational structure. In addition, there may be explicit costs associated with the funds transfers and implicit costs to manage and reconcile.

Zero balancing has the benefit of providing access to organizational cash funds that can then he deployed for the best available return - paying down debt or payment against a line of credit, for example.

## Controlled Disbursement

Controlled disbursement is a service used specifically for cash disbursements. Each morning, banks provide their controlled disbursement customers with information about checks to be presented that day, allowing customers to forecast with accuracy the check clearings to occur and the necessary funding that is required for the account. Participating U.S. banks offer controlled disbursement accounts that arc funded once per day. The funding covers all the checks to be cleared on that business day. Those banks that are part of the cash disbursement program will receive a second presentment and therefore provide a second update to bank customers using controlled disbursement services.

## Pooling

Pooling refers to bank services that aggregate cash from various hank accounts, either on a notional or actual basis. To facilitate pooling, credit facilities may need to be arranged to cover debit balances with-in the pooled accounts. Pooling is common in Europe where many cross-border transactions utilize the same currency due to the introduction of the euro. Pooling is relatively straightforward within one country, although legal rules may still restrict its use. However, trans-border pooling is more complex, as countries' individual legal and tax rules may limit or prohibit certain aspects of pooling. Some countries prohibit pooling altogether.

The company's ability to do physical versus notional pooling depends on local country regulations and the corporate legal structure.

Physical pooling means that funds are actually moved from pooling accounts into the central ac-count. Notional pooling means that funds are not actually transferred, but balance and transaction data are reported as if transfers had taken place. In addition, interest is calculated as if transfers had occurred. The term pooling is also used to refer to an organizational strategy where a central treasury acts as an in-house bank to other parts of the organization. Some countries prohibit or restrict intercompany transactions, including cash pooling. As a result, expert assistance is necessary in this area, since tax and legal issues should be determined prior to engaging in such transactions.

**Lockboxes**

Lockboxes are locations where payments, particularly checks, are collected. Lockboxes provide a number of advantages for receiving payments, including faster processing of receipts, potential for reduced float, and the reporting done by the lockbox provider. There are two major types of lockboxes - wholesale and retail.

**Whole sale and retail lockboxes**

Wholesale lockboxes are used for business-to-business payments. Retail lockboxes are used for consumer payments with high volumes but smaller dollar amounts. Due to their higher volumes, they typically have more rigorous processing requirements. Hybrid lockboxes with attributes of each also exist.

## Global cash management

Companies can also adopt global cash management approaches. However, global cash management adds a layer of complexity to the cash management process. In addition to the issues of forecasting, control, and liquidity, legal and regulatory issues may affect an organization's cash management. At present, a handful of major financial institutions dominate the global cash management business, handling the bulk of global regional and global cash management. There are a number of techniques and bank services for consolidating and managing cash between accounts, financial institutions, both domestically and cross border. However, even in jurisdictions with a common currency, such as the euro zone, there can be difficulties consolidating cash seamlessly.

## Cash management of cross-border transactions

Cross-border transactions, even in the same currency, may have legal, regulatory, or tax implications. Such transactions, therefore, require the expertise of a professional who is well versed in the country and cross-border specifics. One major consideration with global cash management is in the area of electronic payments. In addition to the vast differences between countries, in many countries, checks are not widely used, and in some countries, they are almost nonexistent. For example, many European countries have a very high level of maturity with electronic payments. Although national automated clearinghouse payment systems exist, the trend appears to be toward international payments linkages. Pooling is a technique to notionally or physically aggregate cash between different parts of an organization. Excess funds can he used to offset a deficit in other accounts. On a daily basis, positive and negative balances are aggregated, and interest earned or due is calculated.

Typically, for pooling techniques to work well, bank accounts at the same bank and credit facilities may be required. Although intuitively appealing, pooling can present logistical complexities due to legal and regulatory environments in other countries. Zero balancing, which is commonly used in the United States, can also be used in global cash management. In a zero-balancing arrangement, accounts with excess funds are used to fund accounts with a deficit, provided that accounts are within the same bank and country. Subsidiaries use their own accounts, and transfers into and out of the master account helps fund them.

**Clearing and Settlement of Payments**

Clearing is the process of transmitting, reconciling, and, in some cases, confirming payment orders prior to settlement. It can also include the netting instructions (the offsetting of several positions or obligations between trading partners or participants) and the establishment of final positions for settlement. Settlement is the discharging of obligations related to payment transactions between two or more parties.

**Wire Payment Checklist**

Payment via a wire transfer is one of the most popular modes of settling obligations. To avoid errors causing transferred payments to be returned the information included in the wire transfer transmission should be accurate and complete. The following wire payment checklist of information should be provided by the sending organization in order to ensure timely delivery of funds via wire transfer:

• Name, address, and account number of sender

• Name and account number of recipient

• Recipient's financial institution

• Branch number (transit number) of recipient's financial institution (the branch where the account is actually held)

• Amount of payment

• Payment value date

• Information regarding the details of the remittance, such as invoices paid or reference numbers.

Recipients have a role too. Wire transfer recipients, on their part, should take several steps, including:

• A discussion should be initiated with the organization's financial institution prior to receiving transfers, if possible.

• Ensure that the financial institution has specific instructions as to notifying the organization about in-coming funds and how remittance information included with the funds transfer is to be treated.

- The recipient should also ensure that the sender has complete information, including correct corporate or organizational name, name of the receiving financial institution, account number, and transit or branch number

**Cash Management Checklist**

Many activities can be used by the company Treasurer to improve cash management practices and consequently the cash position. The following practices are often useful:

**Receipts and Disbursement related Practices**

- Cash collected as quickly as possible
- Disbursement payments delayed as long as possible without violating supplier and vendor relationships

**Staff-Related Cash Management Practices**

- Comprehensive controls to protect cash assets and payments from theft and fraudulent activity
- Knowledgeable, well-rounded staff
- Clear division of duties
- Appropriate compensation structure

**Cash Flow Forecasting Practices**

- Cash forecast regularly updated
- Cash forecast rolling forward

- Automation of regular cash flow forecast items such as pay-roll, lease payments, and so forth
- Automation of routine processes, such as downloads of hank balance and transaction data
- Ad hoc management reporting
- Information available based on different criteria and detail
- Different views of cash flow data

## Cash Management Activities and Practices

- Integrated view of cash management across the organization.
- Timely and accurate information from other parts of the organization that affect cash flows
- Involvement of accounting, audit, and legal professionals
- Clear audit trail

## Liquidity and Cash Management

Liquidity is the ability of an organization to meet its short-term financial obligations. Successful organizations must maintain a balance between underutilized cash balances and adequate short-term resources to conduct day-to-day operations. These are some of the challenges of liquidity management. Liquidity management encompasses the management of cash balances, including short-term funding and investments for excess cash.

The availability or otherwise, of alternatives for raising cash during temporary shortages and the existence of opportunities to invest excess cash at its disposal on a short-term basis are important to the functioning of an organization. Liquidity and resultant ability of a company to meet its short term financial obligations, is important for several reasons, including:

- o **Opportunities.** It provides the company with the ability to take advantage of opportunities as they arise, for example, for new products, acquisitions, or timely investments in once in a lifetime opportunities.

- o **Future projects**. It facilitates the funding for future projects and acquisitions critical for the company's long-term survival.

- o **Buffer**. Liquidity can serve as a financial buffer against an unexpected decline in revenues or sales thereby enabling the company to ride such short term setbacks.

- o **Collateralization.** The company may need urgent funding through a loan with the lenders insisting on some form of collateral. In this case having liquidity can help the company meet the need for collateral demanded against borrowing or debt issuance.

o **Research and Development**. (R & D). R & D is very important for the survival and long-term competitiveness of any company and yet it tends to be very cash intensive. A company with the necessary liquidity has no problem funding such cash-intensive activities.

The management of cash balances is one of the most critical treasury roles in any organisation. If there is excess cash, the excess funds can be moved into an interest-earning account overnight, or alternatively they can be invested for a longer period of time, depending on the companies, liquidity and working capital needs. In deciding where and how to invest such resources it is important to bear in mind that the treasury's focus with short-term assets such as these is on risk, return, and liquidity. Although cash management focuses on the methods used to make and receive payments, liquidity management focuses on the balances that arise as a result of those transactions. Liquidity management is also closely associated with management of working capital, which includes accounts payable and accounts receivable and ultimately affects liquidity. Accounts payable and receivables management have been discussed, in previous chapters. It should be noted that anything that affects the ability of the organization to fund short-term obligations is potentially within the scope of liquidity management.

There are a number of methods that can be used to measure the effectiveness of liquidity management, including availability of liquidity, working capital ratios, accounts receivables outstanding, and average cash balances, for example. Other issues worthy of consideration with regard to effectiveness of liquidity management include bank charges and costs of funding.

**Money Market**

Money market is one of the avenues that many organizations use to manage excess liquidity in the form of cash and short-term assets. The money market is the wholesale market for cash, liabilities, and short-term fixed income securities. It facilitates short-term investing of excess cash and short-term funding for borrowers. The money market being mostly an institutional market, facilitates management of amounts ranging from about USD 100,000 to many millions of dollars. The maturity of most money market instruments typically range from overnight (one day) to about a year, although longer-term securities may also be used.

**Key Attributes of Money Market Investments**

Money market investments typically meet these attributes:

- They tend to have a relatively short term to maturity
- They are usually low-risk, high-credit quality due to their short duration
- The liquidity requirements of the investments vary depending on the investor; however, as a rule, the requirement is usually for high liquidity.

Like all other securities, money market securities are subject to market risk, primarily interest rate risk, foreign exchange risk (if the securities are foreign currency denominated) and credit risk. Commonly used financial instruments for managing excess short-term cash include bank deposits, bankers' acceptances, certificates of deposit, commercial paper, Treasury bills and other government securities, and money market mutual or pooled funds.

**The Role of Monetary Policy**

Monetary policy in many countries are set through the specialized Open Market Committee set up by the various Central Banks. Open market operations, which are used to manage short-term interest rates within a given target rate, are conducted mostly through repurchase agreements (repos, or sale and repurchase agreements) and the purchase and sale of government securities. Other Central Banks may opt to affects monetary policy primarily through the overnight rate charged between money market dealers. In this case, the Banks maintain the overnight rate within a given band, say, 25 basis point (1/4 percent) band, with the upper band known as the Bank Rate. The target for the overnight rate is the midpoint between the upper and lower bands. The Bank lends at the Bank Rate and pays the bottom of the band on surplus balances for participants.

**Key Money Market Participants and Players**

The money market is, for the most part, a dealer market. Dealers trade among themselves and with customers in a virtual dealer marketplace.

Participants in the money market include banks and other financial institutions, investment dealers, governments, fund managers, insurance companies, and corporations, as well as central banks. Trading may be facilitated by interdealer firms that intermediate transactions between dealers at financial institutions for wholesale amounts.

**Electronic Trades in Money Markets**

One of the phenomenal recent developments is the increasingly, electronic marketplaces that have evolved to facilitate trading in money market securities. Financial institutions, particularly large banks, are active participants in the money market because of their significant cash management requirements that arise as a result of their core business and financial market activities. Smaller financial institutions may focus on liquidity and interest rate risk management, while larger financial institutions employ money market traders for proprietary and customer trading within specific areas of expertise. In large trading rooms, money market traders specialize in particular markets or instruments, such as government debt (e.g., Treasury bills) and short-term corporate debt (e.g., commercial paper), foreign exchange, and various types of derivatives.

**The Role of Governments, Government Agencies and Corporates in Money Market**

Governments and their agencies incur obligations at various levels of government from the national level down to the municipal or county level, and they similarly issue debt to support their activities and finance both short-and long-term shortfalls. Governments and their agencies may be both issuers of and investors in money market securities. Corporations and related companies make up the last major tier of money market participants, both as issuers and as investors. Although some corporations are small money market investors, others are extremely large and sophisticated, and their portfolios may rival or even surpass those of some financial institutions. It is not uncommon for corporations to use the services of financial institutions to bundle and package assets for security creation, such as is usually done in the securitization market. In addition, corporations may also issue their own obligations through debt issues in order to raise the required funding.

**Key Features and Basics of the Current Money Markets**

It is important to note that money market securities are usually fixed income securities with short-term maturities. As such, they provide contractual payments in the form of interest which may be payable periodically or on maturity and return of principal to investors. Most money market securities mature in under a one year, although the investment universe may include securities of slightly longer maturity and some, such as mutual funds, have no maturity date.

**Nominal Interest Rates**

Nominal interest rates consist of a lending rate for money, plus an inflation component and a credit component. Because most money market securities are relatively short term in nature, inflation is less of an issue than credit. The quality of investment depends on the likelihood of repayment and therefore the creditworthiness of the issuer. The higher the credit rating, all else being equal, the lower the yield. The downgrading or otherwise altering of an issuer's credit rating can have a significant effect on its ability to sell debt securities. Most money market securities pay interest at maturity. A few have periodic interest, either because they mature in more than one year or because the original issue had coupon payments.

**Discount and Interest Bearing Securities**

Money market instruments are either discount or interest bearing. Discount bearing instruments are sold at discount and mature at their par or face value. The difference is interest income to the investor. Interest-bearing instruments are similar in nature to a bank deposit, where a face or par amount is invested and it earns income which is paid at maturity. Money market instruments generally do not coupon interest or periodic interest payments. Instead, interest is usually at maturity, and most instruments mature in under one year. Most money market trading is for same-day settlement, although the specifics vary by country and sometimes by instrument. Next-day trading is also available.

Fixed income securities with longer original trading terms to maturity may settle three business days after trade date (T+3). There have been initiatives aimed at reducing settlement time for fixed income and equity securities from T+3 to T+1. However these have been sidelined as of the present. Money market dealers and customers are linked by telephone and

126

electronic dealing systems. A basic trading protocol exists in the money market as well as in other types of trading. When two-sided (bid and offer) prices are given, the dealer making the price, known as the price maker has the right to the favorable price or rate. In the money market, where price and interest rate are inversely related, this means the price taker, the dealer requesting a price borrows at the higher rate (lower price) and invests at the lower interest rate (higher price). This protocol exists when banks and dealers trade with one another, as well as when they trade with their customers.

## Investing in Government Securities

In the United States, the most common government securities are Treasury bills, which are discount obligations issued by the U.S. Treasury. These short-term federal government obligations traditionally offer the lowest return and are considered to be very low risk. They are issued weekly through an auction process, with regular maturities. Securities issued by a government agency include bonds issued by Federal National Mortgage Association (FNMA, or commonly known as Fannie Mae), Government National Mortgage Association (GNMA, or commonly known as Ginnie Mae). Although generally grouped with government securities, these agency securities are not explicitly guaranteed by the U.S. government. Municipal bonds are issued by city and community governments in two types: general obligation bonds and revenue bonds.

## Certificates of Deposit

Certificates of deposit (CDs) are interest bearing and may be negotiable or non-negotiable. Most money market CDs are negotiable and traded in the secondary market. There are several types defined by interest rate type or currency, the issuer and where issued. Based on interest type we have fixed rate and variable rate CDs. In the case of fixed rate CDs the interest rate is set for term of the CD with the borrower paying periodic interest if maturity is greater than one year. And with variable CDs interest rate is reset on a predetermined frequency, for example, monthly or quarterly. Based on currency the most common CDs are Eurocurrency CDs meaning CDs issued outside the domicile of the issuers in the issuers currency. So Eurodollar CDs, for example, constitute CDs issued by financial institutions outside the United States in U.S. dollars. Second currency type CD is the Yankee CDs which are issued in U.S. dollars by foreign banks operating in the United States.

## Understanding the Eurocurrency Market

This should not to be confused with the euro, the currency adopted by a dozen European nations in economic union, the term Eurocurrency refers to currency deposits held by banks outside the country's borders. For example, Eurodollars are dollar-denominated deposits held by a bank outside the United States. Similarly, Euroyen are yen deposits held by a bank outside Japan. However, the name is a bit of a misnomer. Although the bank holding the deposits is outside the country, the currency itself is placed on the bank's behalf with correspondent banks in the country. The traditional (and largest) market for Eurocurrencies is London. London is a geographically central location and a major center of trading activity.

## Bankers' Acceptances

Bankers' acceptances (BAs) are issues of corporate debt that have been accepted (guaranteed) by a bank. Due to the guarantee issued by the bank against the debt the BAs are very popular with investors. BAs are created when a bank lends to a corporation, adding its own guarantee. The newly issued BA is then sold to investors. For smaller amounts of debt, or issuance by companies whose names are not well known, the issuance of BAs is an alternative for raising short-term funds. BAs often are used in financing of import/ export transactions. Although these securities originate as corporate debt they are guaranteed ("accepted") by a financial institution and become a liability of the financial institution. As a result, although they are originated through corporate indebtedness, they are properly classified as bank obligations and trade in the market on the strength of the bank giving the guarantee. In the United States, BAs are issued most often as a result of trade transactions.

## Commercial Paper

This is one of the most common corporate money market securities. Commercial paper issues are usually unsecured debt issued by companies wishing to borrow from the market. The companies issuing commercial paper are normally relatively well known. Most commercial paper are actually short term securities and matures in 30 days or so. Although it is possible to find commercial paper with maturities exceeding 30 days it is very rare that they exceed 270 days due to registration requirements by securities regulators which many issuers tend to wish to avoid. In other words in many jurisdictions 270 days is the maximum maturity permissible without registration of the Commercial Paper by the relevant securities exchange.

**The Distinction between Primary and Secondary Securities**

Market Money market securities are often offered to investors through the wide distribution networks of investment dealers and financial institutions. Dealers can act as principals, buying the issue and selling it to earn a profit, or as agents. In addition, many issuers sell debt issues directly to their investor community, such as the direct commercial paper issuers. When a money market security is issued initially, it is said to be a primary market transaction, as the security is created and sold initially. Each time the security is sold thereafter, it is said to be trading in the secondary market. Once the debt has been sold by the issuer, it trades in the secondary market, and it may be bought and sold dozens of times before its maturity.

**Asset-Backed Securities**

Asset-backed securities are a growing class of securities that often are created through securitization activities. In securitization, a pool of assets such as consumer loans, are packaged together, along with additional credit enhancements, and sold to investors.

Asset-backed securities may be structured as trusts, and the investors receive returns that are generally slightly more attractive than other money market securities. Asset-backed securities are used to repackage auto loans, credit card receivables, and mortgages, among other things. It is important to assess the attributes of each issue, including credit enhancement techniques and legal issues.

**Use of Foreign Exchange Swaps for Cash Management**

Foreign exchange swaps are commonly used for cash management purposes, particularly within large organizations that have cash management requirements in several currencies. Due to the fact that foreign exchange is also a key business of financial institutions, trading in foreign exchange and foreign exchange swaps is common. Foreign exchange swaps, provide the link between foreign exchange and money markets. Not to be confused with longer-term currency and interest rate swaps, a foreign exchange swap consists of a spot transaction with a simultaneously arranged forward transaction. Currencies are exchanged at both the spot date and the forward date. Since the spot and forward rates are set at the time of the transaction, the difference between the two rates reflects the interest differential between the two currencies over the term of the swap. The result is the ability to use the foreign exchange markets to borrow and lend currencies, augmenting other money market transactions.

Three major types of foreign exchange swaps are used for cash management purposes, depending on the start date of the swap. Foreign exchange swaps may be transacted beginning the same day (cash value), the next business day or "tom-next" (local spot value), or two business days or "spot-next" (international spot value). Amounts transacted normally required to be wholesale amounts of at least USD 5 million or more, but much larger amounts are not uncommon.

**Other Types of Securities in the Money Market**

The money market also contains securities with call or retraction features. Originally issued as longer-term securities, as their maturity approaches, they may become potential money market investments. A callable security allows the issuer to retire the security at a pre-determined call price and date. Call features are attractive to debt issuers because they enablable the issuer to refinance at a lower interest rate, should interest rates decline. Normally a minimum holding period is provided for the investor before the security can be called away by the issuer. A fixed income instrument may have a call schedule consisting of several call dates and prices throughout its life. Generally, the earlier in its maturity it is called, the greater the call premium paid to the investor. It is important to be aware of all the attributes of securities before they are selected for a portfolio, whether a money market or term portfolio. For callable securities, this would include the next call price and date, subsequent call prices and dates, and notice requirement. Knowing this will enable the investor to assess the likelihood of a call occurring and therefore the relative attractiveness of holding the security. Investors may choose callable securities despite their being likely to be called; if they deem their credit quality and yield to call is attractive enough as compared to alternatives available in the market.

Other securities include retractable securities and those with periodic interest rate resets.

## Money Market Mutual or Pooled Funds

Mutual or pooled funds are a fairly recent development in many countries. They constitute portfolios of securities in which investors hold units or shares, as an investment vehicle. Normally the value of these units fluctuate with the net asset value of the underlying assets, but many funds holding money market securities set the net asset value at a fixed (but not guaranteed) net asset value. Money market funds are popular with money market investors because of their convenience. One of the advantages to mutual funds is that reporting, management, and analysis are also outsourced. Many funds offer excellent liquidity, although some planning and cash flow forecasting is necessary. In addition, funds may offer attractive cutoff times for new money, which may enable treasury to complete the day's transactions before rolling excess cash into a fund. The organization using money market funds should ensure that the funds are managed in a style that is appropriate for the investing organization. Considerations include the investment style, types of limits employed such as credit limits, whether leverage is utilized, and whether securities lending is used. It is also necessary to assess what access to funds exists under volatile market conditions. Fund managers may be able to defer redemptions under such conditions.

**Short-term Investment Management**

The existence of a short-term money market portfolio offers several advantages to the organization, including:

- Meeting the need for liquidity within the organization to take advantage of opportunities as they arise, or to fund future specific projects or acquisitions, for example
- Providing an opportunity to earn investment income; even with relatively low interest rates, this can be significant in a large organization
- Creating a buffer against more risky business activities, as may be the case during the early or growth phase of a company
- Meeting the need for collateral, if any, for future borrowing or financing activities.

Money market investment management can be undertaken using two main approaches - an active or passive approach. The decision on the best approach depends on the type of organization, management's intentions, internal policies, the financial management team, and the portfolio itself, including size, composition, purpose, and so on. An actively managed money market portfolio attempts to create additional returns for the organization. However, it is important to note that, in attempting to out-perform, the portfolio will incur additional risk that may ultimately result in poorer than average results.

Management must be comfortable with the increased risk that results from an increased performance objective targets, involving for example, outperforming the market, otherwise it should not go this route. More passive approaches to cash management may result in something similar to the market rate of return, less management costs. A passive portfolio management strategy attempts to track a benchmark rate of return, while looking for protection against adverse market movements rather than trying to outperform the overall trend of the market. Passive portfolio management techniques, typically involve lower levels of risk because they utilize strategies that are not attempting to outperform the market.

Regardless of the type of investment management strategy pursued, money market assets are valuable to the organization. It is therefore very important that their management is outlined in a clearly formulated investment policy and the ramifications of the investment style adopted understood and formally sanctioned by senior management and the board of directors of the company. The adopted investment management policy must be rigorously monitored and managed via the company's Asset and Liabilities Committee or such similar specialized committee

## Passive Techniques for Short-term Investment

The most common passive techniques for, short-term investment management involves creating a maturity ladder as the basis of investment in securities and matching which involves matching the maturity date of the securities to the date when the funds will be required by the company. Both are relatively low analysis and low cost to implement, because no interest rate forecasting is involved. However, it is important to note that even with relatively passive investment management techniques, credit analysis is still an ongoing critical part of the process.

## Investing through a Maturity Ladder

With a maturity ladder, funds are invested in money market securities or deposits with consecutive rollover or maturity dates. Suppose a corporate investor has a small amount of cash that management wants to invest. No liquidity is expected to be required for at least one month, and the maximum investment term based on the cash forecast is three months. The company uses a laddering strategy. The funds available are divided into three approximately equal amounts. A third is invested in a one-month deposit, another third in two-month deposit, and the remainder in a three-month deposit. As each maturity occurs, the deposit is rolled over into a three-month maturity. The result is that every month a maturing deposit is available for liquidity purposes. In addition, the organization takes -advantage of the slightly higher interest rates that are typically avail-able for three-month deposits as compared with one-month deposits.

Of course, the strategy might not be appropriate if management believed that interest rates were likely to move higher in the near term. In addition, such a strategy presumes an upward-sloping yield curve, in which higher yields are available for longer maturities. This is not always the case.

**Matching Maturity Dates**

Matching maturity dates of securities to specific cash flow requirement dates is a passive technique for short-term investing. Where funds are designated for a specific purpose, passive techniques such as matching are a good and viable alternative. Rather than forecast future interest rates, investing decisions are made based on the most appropriate maturity date, within defined limits and parameters. The maturity date for new securities is chosen if possible, for its match with the expected requirement date for funds. The advantage of matching is that it is relatively easy to implement and does not require active forecasting of interest rates or the yield curve. The corollary is that the performance of the portfolio will reflect the average maturity of the instruments in it which are dictated by the organisation's requirements for cash. In addition, if there is a great deal of forecast uncertainty, investments will necessarily be of shorter maturity than they otherwise would be to take the uncertainty into account. In a normal, upward-sloping yield curve environment, this means that yield will be lower for shorter maturity dates.

**The Role of Outsourcing in Money Market Investment**

Some companies may opt for the outsourcing of money market investment management as an alternative especially where the companies that do not have the interest or internal resources to manage short term funds in-house. Different approaches to of outsourcing can be pursued, including investing funds with professional money managers or in money market mutual funds, for example. Although outsourcing often is considered to be a passive strategy, its style as passive or active more properly depends on how the funds are managed. One reason why companies adopt the outsourcing alternative is because, in many cases, cost savings can be achieved through outsourcing. For example, some not-for-profit organizations obtain very attractive pricing on pooled or mutual funds that create a compelling argument for outsourcing. Many funds offer institutional pricing for large dollar amounts with significantly lower fees.

**Active Techniques for Making Money Market Investments**

There are two major categories of active techniques for money market investment management. The first includes strategies that involve anticipating changes in interest rates or the yield curve. The second method for active investment management focuses on altering credit quality, or alternatively anticipating a change in credit quality. Although, in theory, this method of investment management could be augmented by more complex techniques, such as the use of credit derivatives, in practice that is not the case. Active management can also be facilitated with the use of interest rate derivatives, such as forward rate agreements, futures, or options. These are however outside the scope of this book.

The intent of an active investment management strategy is to earn returns that are greater than those otherwise available with more passive strategies. However, if market changes in interest rates, the yield curve, or credit quality, for example, are incorrectly anticipated, lower returns or a loss may result. If derivatives are employed, there is also a potential for trading leverage to be employed, which would com-pound the size of losses, as well as introducing the counterparty risks associated with derivatives.

**Use of Yield Curve Strategies**

Active yield curve strategies anticipate the future structure of the yield curve in order to earn additional return. Riding the yield curve is one such strategy. It involves buying securities with a longer maturity than the required time horizon, with the intent of selling the securities at the required time horizon. In an upward-sloping yield curve environment, as a money instrument approaches maturity, yields on similar instruments decline and prices rise. By selling the security instrument prior to maturity some of this behavior can be exploited.

Depending on the behavior of interest rates and yield curve during the life of the security, this may add additional return. Other yield curve strategies take a more specific approach based on the anticipated changes. In addition, some strategies involve interest rate derivatives.

With active strategies, one major risk is that the interest rate forecast does materialize, and the organization earns a lower return than otherwise expected. In addition, as with any strategy, credit risk (and counterparty risk if derivatives are used should be monitored since the advantage of a correct call on interest rates or the yield curve can be erased quickly if the issuer's credit rating is downgraded.

**Credit Strategies**

In general, it is expected that an increase in risk should he accompanied by a commensurate increase in return. Credit strategies are active strategies that attempt to take advantage of the changes in assessed credit quality. For example, if a money market portfolio manager believes that a debt issuer is about to be upgraded, it may be advantageous to buy debt securities from the issuer in anticipation of the upgrade. Prior to an upgrade, prices will be lower as risk, and therefore yield, is considered to be higher. Other credit-related investment strategies involve a reduction in credit quality of holdings in the portfolio in order to increase the yield. In some large organizations, it may be possible to borrow by issuing debt at a better rate than that available from investments. The organization can issue its own debt and use the debt proceeds to invest in slightly lower-quality securities. The spread becomes gross income, from which adjustments for expenses and risk must be taken. There are risks involved with credit-related strategies, including the risk of an incorrect assessment and suffering a credit loss as a result. A credit loss can range from the default of the issuer, which is very serious, to a deterioration in credit quality, which results in capital loss.

For credit strategies to be successful, a manager must be able to correctly assess credit quality independently of the assessments widely available within the market, such as those provided by credit rating agencies. It is noteworthy that the assessment of credit risk is a very complex exercise. However, opportunities for credit strategies may arise from an issuer that is well known to the investor, such as a prime supplier or related company, for whom a credit assessment may not be an issue. It is important to consider that credit quality, however determined, can deteriorate relatively quickly, particularly if there is a concurrent liquidity, economic, or financial event. In addition, the assessments provided by credit rating agencies or independent assessment, although very useful, are not infallible. Therefore, an organization pursuing credit strategies must be comfortable with the additional risks that such strategies involve.

## Management of the Money Market Portfolio and Strategic Issues

A clear articulation of the objectives of the money market portfolio, as well as the organization's resources and risk tolerance, will help to determine the most appropriate management strategies the company should pursue. If an active money market investment strategy is planned, it is important to ensure that staff members have the time, market data, and knowledge they need to effectively implement such a strategy.

The investment policy adopted by the organization should detail the objectives of the management of the money market portfolio as clearly as possible. Other important issues that must be considered in the articulated policy include more availability of credit lines, dealer relationships, and portfolio management analytics. Active portfolio management strategies typically require greater information and analytics to price individual securities, test strategies and scenarios, monitor credit developments, review changes to the portfolio, and measure and report risk and performance. This information requires analytical systems as well as appropriate control processes, both of which can add costs to the management of the portfolio. If treasury staff members are required to manage additional functions, areas of responsibility may suffer from increased demands or additional personnel may be required. Active management requires additional time on the part of management, who must be cognizant of the risks and develop an appropriate risk management and oversight strategy that is consistent with the organization's governance. If several currencies have material cash flows, it may be necessary to manage portfolios in more than the domestic or operating currency. Doing this may require additional dealer relationships and analytics.

The expected time availability for the funds may make it easier to defend a passive strategy where the security's maturity matches the requirement for funds.

## Benchmarking Money Market Portfolios

Benchmarking money market portfolio returns involves comparing risk and returns to an external reference or benchmark rate to assess the portfolio's performance. Performance measurement is the completion of the investment cycle that includes developing policy, implementation, and performance reporting. Many money market portfolios are benchmarked against published money market indices. Composite indices can also he created based on portfolio target asset allocation, such as commercial paper or T-bills. Libor (London Interbank Offered Rate) is also used as a benchmark rate. The benchmark should be representative of the portfolio holdings.

## Money Market Investment Policy

Money market investing is intended to maximize returns on short-term assets and protect them from market risk and credit risk. The key attributes that must be managed are risk, return, and liquidity. These three attributes work together. For example, it is usually necessary to increase risk or sacrifice liquidity to increase return. In general, short-term portfolios are more risk averse than longer-term portfolios because they have less time to recover from financial market ups and downs. The investment policy provides specific direction on the methods that should be taken by an organization in its achievement of these attributes in its money market investment activities. In doing so, it provides a clear statement of portfolio objectives and constraints. The policy also provides treasury staff and management with a mandate, which avoids judgment of investment decisions by hindsight.

Although there are many variations, a money market investment policy typically covers these areas at a minimum:

**Setting the Objectives for the Portfolio**

The objectives are usually set around:

- **Risk.** Appropriate for the portfolio and the objectives - most a low-level risk for short-term liquidity
- **Liquidity.** Appropriate for the portfolio and the objectives commonly a high level of liquidity is sought
- **Return.** Appropriate for the portfolio and the objectives normally secondary to risk and liquidity

**Standards of Care Applicable to the Portfolio's Management**

- Prudence in the management of the portfolio, including use of judgment and care Potential conflicts of interest and ethical considerations
- Authority and its delegation

**Requirements for Custodial Service Providers, and Issuers**

In this regard the investment policy usually defines clearly:

- Internal control issues that have to be applied in order to protect funds from errors or frauds and appropriate checks and balances that must be exercised to prevent unauthorized or fraudulent transactions

- Authorization of financial institutions, dealers, or custodians including information and authorities required before any transaction is undertaken
- Minimum credit quality of, usually in terms of ratings, counterparties, issuers and custodians

## Permitted Types of Investment Securities

- Government securities (e.g., Treasury bills)
- Supranational Issues, if appropriate
- Corporate securities, if applicable
- Commercial paper, if appropriate
- Certificates of deposit, if appropriate
- Other securities that are appropriate given the organization's objectives and constraints

## Constraints on the Portfolio and Individual Securities

- Maximum dollar or percentage limit permitted to be invested in debt and liabilities of individual issuers
- Maximum dollar or percentage limit that can be invested by type of securities
- Maximum term to maturity allowed for individual investments
- Requirements for diversification in terms duration or proportions and combinations
- Permitted use of derivatives, if any, and restrictions

- Required action if credit quality declines or there are limit breaches
- Maximum dollar amount maturing on a given day

**Reporting Requirements and Review Processes for the Portfolio**

- Methodology for calculating and reporting portfolio performance
- Benchmarks for the various portfolio asset classes
- Frequency of repricing at current market prices (marking-to-market)
- Frequency and process for policy review and update
- Requirements for controls and audit
- Any other constraints or requirements

**Managing Cash Shortfalls**

Temporary cash shortfalls are a normal part of operations for many organizations. If there is a cash shortfall or negative balance, it may be necessary to arrange funding, such as a drawdown on the organization's operating line of credit, prime loan, arrangement of short-term bor. rowing with a lender, or the issuance of short-term debt such as bankers' acceptances or commercial paper. Strategies to fund cash shortfalls typically meet these attributes:

- Short term in nature and can be repaid easily or rolled over, as necessary, for flexibility

- Cheap to issue without significant regulatory hurdles, conditions or costs
- Quick and easy to issue and ideally can be issued in course of a telephone call or two
- Once the initial setup has been undertaken, the issuance of debt such as commercial paper or bankers' acceptances or a drawdown on the organization's line of credit, can be facilitated. In most cases, agreements are in place in advance of the requirement for funding.

**Debt Issuance.** Debt securities, such as commercial paper or bankers' acceptances, can be issued to meet a demand for short-term funding. Where short-term securities are issued regularly, there may loyal investor demand for securities. In this case, it may be worthwhile to issue securities regularly to maintain the favorable investor community and market for the debt. As a result, debt issuance may occur when there is not an anticipated cash shortfall. If borrowing can be done at a lower rate than that available on appropriate risk securities, excess funds can be reinvested.

**Receivables Financing.** Accounts receivables financing is an alternative for financing short-term cash requirements. Also known as factoring, receivables financing may be with or without recourse. With recourse financing, which is lower cost, the lender collects from the receivables customer. The borrower is liable to the lender if the customer defaults. With nonrecourse financing, which is more expensive, the lender collects from the receivables customer. If the customer defaults, the lender suffers the loss. A similar type of asset financing is based on company inventory.

## Securitization as a Financing Mechanism

Securitization is one of the approaches often used for financing in specialized areas. Securitization involves bundling and packaging a pool of assets (e.g., customer loans) and issuing securities backed by the assets. Credit enhancement is used to make the securities more attractive and therefore more salable to various types of investors. Complexities, including credit enhancement and legal fees, can add significant costs to these securitization structures, which may result in them being less appropriate for short-term temporary funding.

## Short - term Funding via Lines of Credit

Lines credit provide short-term funding up to a maximum amount and term. Offered by financial institutions, they are commonly used for financing short-term cash requirements. Lines of credit provide borrowers with access to funds up to a maximum (the credit limit) for a period of time, and they are popular due to their ease of use and simplicity. Lines may be secured with collateral, such as accounts receivable, or unsecured and granted on the general credit quality of the borrower. Revolving lines of credit can be drawn down and repaid as frequently as desired, to the maximum credit limit. Borrowers should be aware that lines of credit may require payment of a commitment fee to keep the line available, which may be required whether the line is used or not. In addition, restrictions may prevent a line of credit from having an outstanding balance maintained through-out the year. As a result, for organizations that use their line of credit regularly, it may be necessary to pay it down in its entirety at least once per year for a minimum specific term (a cleanup period) according to the terms of the agreement. Doing this helps to assure the lender that the line of credit is not being used for long-term financing. In addition, if funding is based on the availability of a line of cred-it, changes at the lending financial institution may cause the line of credit to not be renewed. In this case, the organization may have to find alternative sources of credit.

Made in United States
North Haven, CT
01 May 2025

68483700R00083